Role Call
JOURNAL
STOP WINGING IT & START **WINNING**

She COLLECTIVE

A bedtime journal to brain dump, reflect, and evaluate your most important roles in life.

First Edition

Copyright © 2021
She Collective Co., LLC

All rights reserved.

ISBN: 979-8-9853152-0-2

No part of this book may be reproduced or transmitted in any form or by ay means, electronic or mechanical, including photocopying, recording or by an information storage and retrieval system – except by a reviewer who may quotebrief passages in a review to be printed in a magazine, newspaper or on the Web – without permission in writing from the publisher.

Design by Margaret Cogswell
www.margaretcogswell.com

She
COLLECTIVE

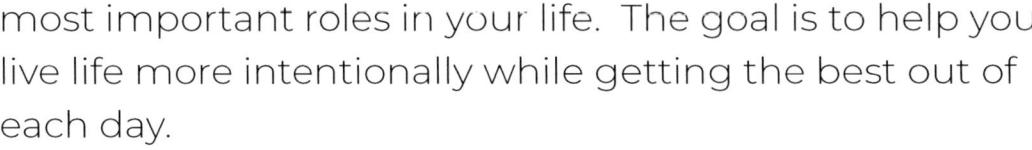

Hi There!

This **90** day Role Journal is to help you prioritize the most important roles in your life. The goal is to help you live life more intentionally while getting the best out of each day.

We are so pumped for you to bring more harmony to your roles. Throughout the past few years, we've really set intentions with our biggest priorities to help us navigate different seasons and schedules.

We've been able to build dreams while keeping our other roles a priority. This reflection journal seeks to help you figure out your top five roles in life. These roles might change with time and that's for you to figure out.

As you keep your top five in mind, you can reflect and

gauge how each role is doing. We have found that it's been really helpful to set goals, list the gratitude and find ways to grow in each area. Evaluating your roles can help you have the best yeses and create boundaries and prioritize your time better.

For example, if a role you have is (MOM), you might set a growth goal for spending less time on your phone while your kids are around. Each night, while you unwind, give yourself grace and remind yourself of the joy you got from that day.

This ROLE CALL Journal is to help you get all your thoughts, dreams, to-dos out while thinking about what you're excited about, what you're grateful for, and what you're enjoying.

This is our only life. Let's live it well. Let's live it fulfilled. Let's seek to grow while celebrating how we lived out our day.

Be proud. Be proud of how far you've come. Be proud of yourself now. And be so proud of where you're going.

Living intentionally will help you with every area of your life. Let's get started!

The COLLECTIVE

ROLE CALL

EXAMPLE

Role: *Mom*

WHAT I AM GRATEFUL FOR ABOUT THIS ROLE
We got to spend time together at the zoo.

WHAT I ENJOYED MOST ABOUT THIS ROLE TODAY
Going on an adventure outside the house.

WHAT I WANT TO DO MORE OF IN THIS ROLE
Plan other adventures.

AREAS TO GROW
Be more present instead of getting household chores done.

Examples of roles are spouse, parent, teacher, health care worker, CEO, business owner, volunteer, friend, sister, daughter, student, athlete, or self.

You are a *woman* that wears many hats, wear them well by taking time each night to reflect.

LIST YOUR TOP ROLES — *Choose Your Top 5*

BRAINDUMP YOUR IDEAS OUT

BEDTIME BRAIN DUMP

- [ ] send email out to new clients
- [ ] renew gym membership
- [ ] return books to the libary
- [ ] schedule doctors appointment
- [ ] clean out pantry
- [ ] make dinner reservation
- [ ] schedule family pictures
- [ ] update family calendar
- [ ] create content for IG
- [ ] make mentoring schedule
- [ ] finish work presentation

GAME PLAN FOR TOMORROW

- workout at 6 am
- shower and get ready
- make breakfast
- throw dinner in the crockpot
- drop kids off at school
- finish to-do list
- make final touches on birthday party

I'M LOOKING FROWARD TO

- the game this weekend
- hanging out with our neighbors
- the cookout in a few weeks
- family vacation
- getting a sitter for date night
- hitting my weightloss goal

Get your thoughts and upcoming to-dos out on paper so you rest your pretty little head knowing you can show up as your best self tomorrow.

YOU ARE A BEAUTIFUL PERSON WITH A BRILLIANT MIND, YOU MATTER.

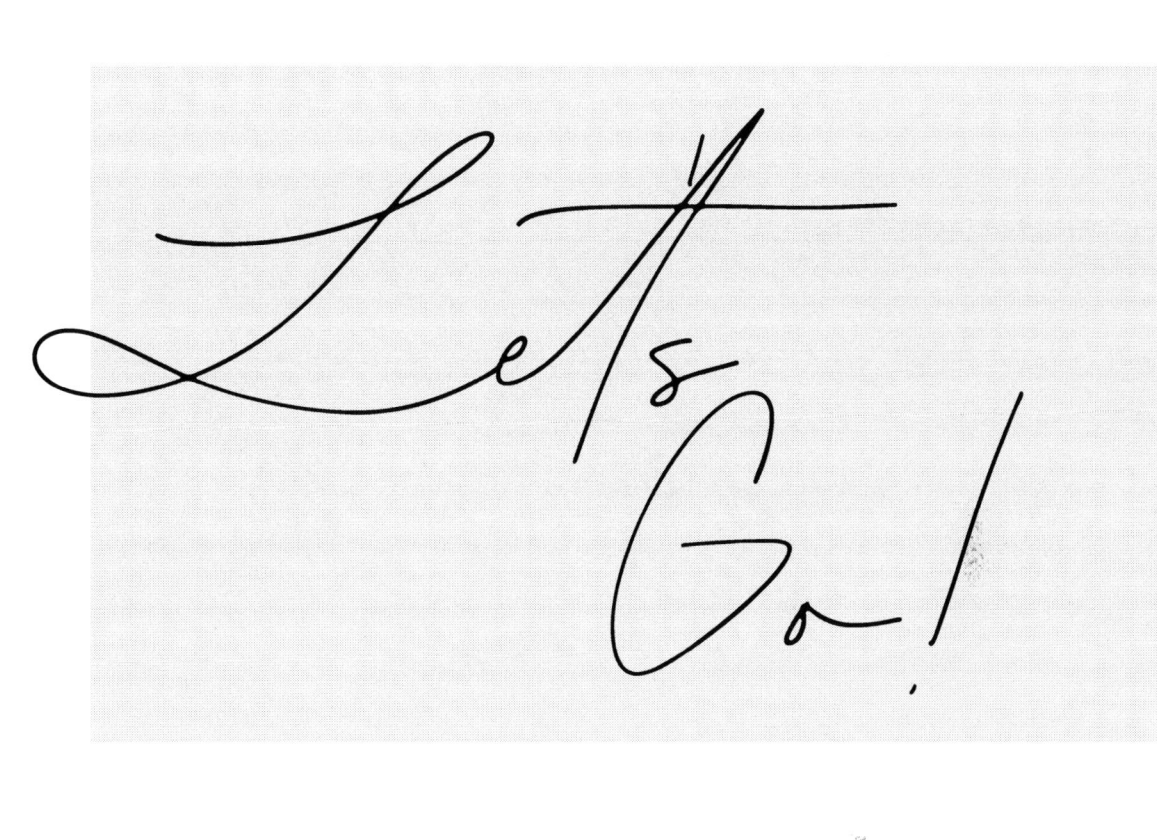

ROLE CALL

Role _____

WHAT I AM GRATEFUL FOR ABOUT THIS ROLE
_____

WHAT I ENJOYED MOST ABOUT THIS ROLE TODAY

WHAT I WANT TO DO MORE OF IN THIS ROLE

AREAS TO GROW
_____

Role _____

WHAT I AM GRATEFUL FOR ABOUT THIS ROLE
_____

WHAT I ENJOYED MOST ABOUT THIS ROLE TODAY

WHAT I WANT TO DO MORE OF IN THIS ROLE

AREAS TO GROW
_____

Role _____

WHAT I AM GRATEFUL FOR ABOUT THIS ROLE
_____

WHAT I ENJOYED MOST ABOUT THIS ROLE TODAY

WHAT I WANT TO DO MORE OF IN THIS ROLE

AREAS TO GROW
_____

Role _____

WHAT I AM GRATEFUL FOR ABOUT THIS ROLE
_____

WHAT I ENJOYED MOST ABOUT THIS ROLE TODAY

WHAT I WANT TO DO MORE OF IN THIS ROLE

AREAS TO GROW
_____

Role _____

WHAT I AM GRATEFUL FOR ABOUT THIS ROLE
_____

WHAT I ENJOYED MOST ABOUT THIS ROLE TODAY

WHAT I WANT TO DO MORE OF IN THIS ROLE

AREAS TO GROW
_____

Bedtime BRAIN DUMP

- [ ] _____
- [ ] _____
- [ ] _____
- [ ] _____
- [ ] _____
- [ ] _____
- [ ] _____
- [ ] _____
- [ ] _____
- [ ] _____
- [ ] _____
- [ ] _____
- [ ] _____

GAME PLAN FOR TOMORROW

_____
_____
_____
_____
_____
_____
_____
_____

I'M LOOKING FORWARD TO

_____
_____
_____
_____
_____
_____
_____
_____

ROLE CALL

Role _____

WHAT I AM GRATEFUL FOR ABOUT THIS ROLE
_____

WHAT I ENJOYED MOST ABOUT THIS ROLE TODAY

WHAT I WANT TO DO MORE OF IN THIS ROLE

AREAS TO GROW
_____

Role _____

WHAT I AM GRATEFUL FOR ABOUT THIS ROLE
_____

WHAT I ENJOYED MOST ABOUT THIS ROLE TODAY

WHAT I WANT TO DO MORE OF IN THIS ROLE

AREAS TO GROW
_____

Role _____

WHAT I AM GRATEFUL FOR ABOUT THIS ROLE
_____

WHAT I ENJOYED MOST ABOUT THIS ROLE TODAY

WHAT I WANT TO DO MORE OF IN THIS ROLE

AREAS TO GROW
_____

Role _____

WHAT I AM GRATEFUL FOR ABOUT THIS ROLE
_____

WHAT I ENJOYED MOST ABOUT THIS ROLE TODAY

WHAT I WANT TO DO MORE OF IN THIS ROLE

AREAS TO GROW
_____

Role _____

WHAT I AM GRATEFUL FOR ABOUT THIS ROLE
_____

WHAT I ENJOYED MOST ABOUT THIS ROLE TODAY

WHAT I WANT TO DO MORE OF IN THIS ROLE

AREAS TO GROW
_____

Bedtime BRAIN DUMP

GAME PLAN FOR TOMORROW

I'M LOOKING FORWARD TO

ROLE CALL

Role _____

WHAT I AM GRATEFUL FOR ABOUT THIS ROLE
_____

WHAT I ENJOYED MOST ABOUT THIS ROLE TODAY

WHAT I WANT TO DO MORE OF IN THIS ROLE

AREAS TO GROW
_____

Role _____

WHAT I AM GRATEFUL FOR ABOUT THIS ROLE
_____

WHAT I ENJOYED MOST ABOUT THIS ROLE TODAY

WHAT I WANT TO DO MORE OF IN THIS ROLE

AREAS TO GROW
_____

Role _____

WHAT I AM GRATEFUL FOR ABOUT THIS ROLE
_____

WHAT I ENJOYED MOST ABOUT THIS ROLE TODAY

WHAT I WANT TO DO MORE OF IN THIS ROLE

AREAS TO GROW
_____

Role _____

WHAT I AM GRATEFUL FOR ABOUT THIS ROLE
_____

WHAT I ENJOYED MOST ABOUT THIS ROLE TODAY

WHAT I WANT TO DO MORE OF IN THIS ROLE

AREAS TO GROW
_____

Role _____

WHAT I AM GRATEFUL FOR ABOUT THIS ROLE
_____

WHAT I ENJOYED MOST ABOUT THIS ROLE TODAY

WHAT I WANT TO DO MORE OF IN THIS ROLE

AREAS TO GROW
_____

ROLE CALL

Role _____

WHAT I AM GRATEFUL FOR ABOUT THIS ROLE
_____

WHAT I ENJOYED MOST ABOUT THIS ROLE TODAY

WHAT I WANT TO DO MORE OF IN THIS ROLE

AREAS TO GROW
_____

Role _____

WHAT I AM GRATEFUL FOR ABOUT THIS ROLE
_____

WHAT I ENJOYED MOST ABOUT THIS ROLE TODAY

WHAT I WANT TO DO MORE OF IN THIS ROLE

AREAS TO GROW
_____

Role _____

WHAT I AM GRATEFUL FOR ABOUT THIS ROLE
_____

WHAT I ENJOYED MOST ABOUT THIS ROLE TODAY

WHAT I WANT TO DO MORE OF IN THIS ROLE

AREAS TO GROW
_____

Role _____

WHAT I AM GRATEFUL FOR ABOUT THIS ROLE
_____

WHAT I ENJOYED MOST ABOUT THIS ROLE TODAY

WHAT I WANT TO DO MORE OF IN THIS ROLE

AREAS TO GROW
_____

Role _____

WHAT I AM GRATEFUL FOR ABOUT THIS ROLE
_____

WHAT I ENJOYED MOST ABOUT THIS ROLE TODAY

WHAT I WANT TO DO MORE OF IN THIS ROLE

AREAS TO GROW
_____

Bedtime BRAIN DUMP

GAME PLAN FOR TOMORROW

I'M LOOKING FORWARD TO

ROLE CALL

Role _____

WHAT I AM GRATEFUL FOR ABOUT THIS ROLE
_____

WHAT I ENJOYED MOST ABOUT THIS ROLE TODAY

WHAT I WANT TO DO MORE OF IN THIS ROLE

AREAS TO GROW
_____

Role _____

WHAT I AM GRATEFUL FOR ABOUT THIS ROLE
_____

WHAT I ENJOYED MOST ABOUT THIS ROLE TODAY

WHAT I WANT TO DO MORE OF IN THIS ROLE

AREAS TO GROW
_____

Role _____

WHAT I AM GRATEFUL FOR ABOUT THIS ROLE
_____

WHAT I ENJOYED MOST ABOUT THIS ROLE TODAY

WHAT I WANT TO DO MORE OF IN THIS ROLE

AREAS TO GROW
_____

Role _____

WHAT I AM GRATEFUL FOR ABOUT THIS ROLE
_____

WHAT I ENJOYED MOST ABOUT THIS ROLE TODAY

WHAT I WANT TO DO MORE OF IN THIS ROLE

AREAS TO GROW
_____

Role _____

WHAT I AM GRATEFUL FOR ABOUT THIS ROLE
_____

WHAT I ENJOYED MOST ABOUT THIS ROLE TODAY

WHAT I WANT TO DO MORE OF IN THIS ROLE

AREAS TO GROW
_____

ROLE CALL

Role _____

WHAT I AM GRATEFUL FOR ABOUT THIS ROLE
_____

WHAT I ENJOYED MOST ABOUT THIS ROLE TODAY

WHAT I WANT TO DO MORE OF IN THIS ROLE

AREAS TO GROW
_____

Role _____

WHAT I AM GRATEFUL FOR ABOUT THIS ROLE
_____

WHAT I ENJOYED MOST ABOUT THIS ROLE TODAY

WHAT I WANT TO DO MORE OF IN THIS ROLE

AREAS TO GROW
_____

Role _____

WHAT I AM GRATEFUL FOR ABOUT THIS ROLE
_____

WHAT I ENJOYED MOST ABOUT THIS ROLE TODAY

WHAT I WANT TO DO MORE OF IN THIS ROLE

AREAS TO GROW
_____

Role _____

WHAT I AM GRATEFUL FOR ABOUT THIS ROLE
_____

WHAT I ENJOYED MOST ABOUT THIS ROLE TODAY

WHAT I WANT TO DO MORE OF IN THIS ROLE

AREAS TO GROW
_____

Role _____

WHAT I AM GRATEFUL FOR ABOUT THIS ROLE
_____

WHAT I ENJOYED MOST ABOUT THIS ROLE TODAY

WHAT I WANT TO DO MORE OF IN THIS ROLE

AREAS TO GROW
_____

Bedtime BRAIN DUMP

GAME PLAN FOR TOMORROW

I'M LOOKING FORWARD TO

ROLE CALL

Role _____

WHAT I AM GRATEFUL FOR ABOUT THIS ROLE
_____

WHAT I ENJOYED MOST ABOUT THIS ROLE TODAY

WHAT I WANT TO DO MORE OF IN THIS ROLE

AREAS TO GROW
_____

Role _____

WHAT I AM GRATEFUL FOR ABOUT THIS ROLE
_____

WHAT I ENJOYED MOST ABOUT THIS ROLE TODAY

WHAT I WANT TO DO MORE OF IN THIS ROLE

AREAS TO GROW
_____

Role _____

WHAT I AM GRATEFUL FOR ABOUT THIS ROLE
_____

WHAT I ENJOYED MOST ABOUT THIS ROLE TODAY

WHAT I WANT TO DO MORE OF IN THIS ROLE

AREAS TO GROW
_____

Role _____

WHAT I AM GRATEFUL FOR ABOUT THIS ROLE
_____

WHAT I ENJOYED MOST ABOUT THIS ROLE TODAY

WHAT I WANT TO DO MORE OF IN THIS ROLE

AREAS TO GROW
_____

Role _____

WHAT I AM GRATEFUL FOR ABOUT THIS ROLE
_____

WHAT I ENJOYED MOST ABOUT THIS ROLE TODAY

WHAT I WANT TO DO MORE OF IN THIS ROLE

AREAS TO GROW
_____

ROLE CALL

Role _____

WHAT I AM GRATEFUL FOR ABOUT THIS ROLE
_____

WHAT I ENJOYED MOST ABOUT THIS ROLE TODAY

WHAT I WANT TO DO MORE OF IN THIS ROLE

AREAS TO GROW
_____

Role _____

WHAT I AM GRATEFUL FOR ABOUT THIS ROLE
_____

WHAT I ENJOYED MOST ABOUT THIS ROLE TODAY

WHAT I WANT TO DO MORE OF IN THIS ROLE

AREAS TO GROW
_____

Role _____

WHAT I AM GRATEFUL FOR ABOUT THIS ROLE
_____

WHAT I ENJOYED MOST ABOUT THIS ROLE TODAY

WHAT I WANT TO DO MORE OF IN THIS ROLE

AREAS TO GROW
_____

Role _____

WHAT I AM GRATEFUL FOR ABOUT THIS ROLE
_____

WHAT I ENJOYED MOST ABOUT THIS ROLE TODAY

WHAT I WANT TO DO MORE OF IN THIS ROLE

AREAS TO GROW
_____

Role _____

WHAT I AM GRATEFUL FOR ABOUT THIS ROLE
_____

WHAT I ENJOYED MOST ABOUT THIS ROLE TODAY

WHAT I WANT TO DO MORE OF IN THIS ROLE

AREAS TO GROW
_____

Bedtime BRAIN DUMP

-
-
-
-
-
-
-
-
-
-
-
-
-
-

GAME PLAN FOR TOMORROW

I'M LOOKING FORWARD TO

ROLE CALL

Role _____

WHAT I AM GRATEFUL FOR ABOUT THIS ROLE
_____

WHAT I ENJOYED MOST ABOUT THIS ROLE TODAY

WHAT I WANT TO DO MORE OF IN THIS ROLE

AREAS TO GROW
_____

Role _____

WHAT I AM GRATEFUL FOR ABOUT THIS ROLE
_____

WHAT I ENJOYED MOST ABOUT THIS ROLE TODAY

WHAT I WANT TO DO MORE OF IN THIS ROLE

AREAS TO GROW
_____

Role _____

WHAT I AM GRATEFUL FOR ABOUT THIS ROLE
_____

WHAT I ENJOYED MOST ABOUT THIS ROLE TODAY

WHAT I WANT TO DO MORE OF IN THIS ROLE

AREAS TO GROW
_____

Role _____

WHAT I AM GRATEFUL FOR ABOUT THIS ROLE
_____

WHAT I ENJOYED MOST ABOUT THIS ROLE TODAY

WHAT I WANT TO DO MORE OF IN THIS ROLE

AREAS TO GROW
_____

Role _____

WHAT I AM GRATEFUL FOR ABOUT THIS ROLE
_____

WHAT I ENJOYED MOST ABOUT THIS ROLE TODAY

WHAT I WANT TO DO MORE OF IN THIS ROLE

AREAS TO GROW
_____

Bedtime BRAIN DUMP

- [ ] _____
- [ ] _____
- [ ] _____
- [ ] _____
- [ ] _____
- [ ] _____
- [ ] _____
- [ ] _____
- [ ] _____
- [ ] _____
- [ ] _____
- [ ] _____
- [ ] _____
- [ ] _____

GAME PLAN FOR TOMORROW

_____
_____
_____
_____
_____
_____
_____
_____

I'M LOOKING FORWARD TO

_____
_____
_____
_____
_____
_____
_____
_____

ROLE CALL

Role _____
WHAT I AM GRATEFUL FOR ABOUT THIS ROLE
_____

WHAT I ENJOYED MOST ABOUT THIS ROLE TODAY | WHAT I WANT TO DO MORE OF IN THIS ROLE

AREAS TO GROW
_____

Role _____
WHAT I AM GRATEFUL FOR ABOUT THIS ROLE
_____

WHAT I ENJOYED MOST ABOUT THIS ROLE TODAY | WHAT I WANT TO DO MORE OF IN THIS ROLE

AREAS TO GROW
_____

Role _____
WHAT I AM GRATEFUL FOR ABOUT THIS ROLE
_____

WHAT I ENJOYED MOST ABOUT THIS ROLE TODAY | WHAT I WANT TO DO MORE OF IN THIS ROLE

AREAS TO GROW
_____

Role _____
WHAT I AM GRATEFUL FOR ABOUT THIS ROLE
_____

WHAT I ENJOYED MOST ABOUT THIS ROLE TODAY | WHAT I WANT TO DO MORE OF IN THIS ROLE

AREAS TO GROW
_____

Role _____
WHAT I AM GRATEFUL FOR ABOUT THIS ROLE
_____

WHAT I ENJOYED MOST ABOUT THIS ROLE TODAY | WHAT I WANT TO DO MORE OF IN THIS ROLE

AREAS TO GROW
_____

Bedtime BRAIN DUMP

GAME PLAN FOR TOMORROW

I'M LOOKING FORWARD TO

ROLE CALL

Role _____

WHAT I AM GRATEFUL FOR ABOUT THIS ROLE
_____

WHAT I ENJOYED MOST ABOUT THIS ROLE TODAY

WHAT I WANT TO DO MORE OF IN THIS ROLE

AREAS TO GROW
_____

Role _____

WHAT I AM GRATEFUL FOR ABOUT THIS ROLE
_____

WHAT I ENJOYED MOST ABOUT THIS ROLE TODAY

WHAT I WANT TO DO MORE OF IN THIS ROLE

AREAS TO GROW
_____

Role _____

WHAT I AM GRATEFUL FOR ABOUT THIS ROLE
_____

WHAT I ENJOYED MOST ABOUT THIS ROLE TODAY

WHAT I WANT TO DO MORE OF IN THIS ROLE

AREAS TO GROW
_____

Role _____

WHAT I AM GRATEFUL FOR ABOUT THIS ROLE
_____

WHAT I ENJOYED MOST ABOUT THIS ROLE TODAY

WHAT I WANT TO DO MORE OF IN THIS ROLE

AREAS TO GROW
_____

Role _____

WHAT I AM GRATEFUL FOR ABOUT THIS ROLE
_____

WHAT I ENJOYED MOST ABOUT THIS ROLE TODAY

WHAT I WANT TO DO MORE OF IN THIS ROLE

AREAS TO GROW
_____

ROLE CALL

Role _____

WHAT I AM GRATEFUL FOR ABOUT THIS ROLE
_____

WHAT I ENJOYED MOST ABOUT THIS ROLE TODAY

WHAT I WANT TO DO MORE OF IN THIS ROLE

AREAS TO GROW
_____

Role _____

WHAT I AM GRATEFUL FOR ABOUT THIS ROLE
_____

WHAT I ENJOYED MOST ABOUT THIS ROLE TODAY

WHAT I WANT TO DO MORE OF IN THIS ROLE

AREAS TO GROW
_____

Role _____

WHAT I AM GRATEFUL FOR ABOUT THIS ROLE
_____

WHAT I ENJOYED MOST ABOUT THIS ROLE TODAY

WHAT I WANT TO DO MORE OF IN THIS ROLE

AREAS TO GROW
_____

Role _____

WHAT I AM GRATEFUL FOR ABOUT THIS ROLE
_____

WHAT I ENJOYED MOST ABOUT THIS ROLE TODAY

WHAT I WANT TO DO MORE OF IN THIS ROLE

AREAS TO GROW
_____

Role _____

WHAT I AM GRATEFUL FOR ABOUT THIS ROLE
_____

WHAT I ENJOYED MOST ABOUT THIS ROLE TODAY

WHAT I WANT TO DO MORE OF IN THIS ROLE

AREAS TO GROW
_____

Bedtime BRAIN DUMP

GAME PLAN FOR TOMORROW

I'M LOOKING FORWARD TO

ROLE CALL

Role _____

WHAT I AM GRATEFUL FOR ABOUT THIS ROLE
_____

WHAT I ENJOYED MOST ABOUT THIS ROLE TODAY

WHAT I WANT TO DO MORE OF IN THIS ROLE

AREAS TO GROW
_____

Role _____

WHAT I AM GRATEFUL FOR ABOUT THIS ROLE
_____

WHAT I ENJOYED MOST ABOUT THIS ROLE TODAY

WHAT I WANT TO DO MORE OF IN THIS ROLE

AREAS TO GROW
_____

Role _____

WHAT I AM GRATEFUL FOR ABOUT THIS ROLE
_____

WHAT I ENJOYED MOST ABOUT THIS ROLE TODAY

WHAT I WANT TO DO MORE OF IN THIS ROLE

AREAS TO GROW
_____

Role _____

WHAT I AM GRATEFUL FOR ABOUT THIS ROLE
_____

WHAT I ENJOYED MOST ABOUT THIS ROLE TODAY

WHAT I WANT TO DO MORE OF IN THIS ROLE

AREAS TO GROW
_____

Role _____

WHAT I AM GRATEFUL FOR ABOUT THIS ROLE
_____

WHAT I ENJOYED MOST ABOUT THIS ROLE TODAY

WHAT I WANT TO DO MORE OF IN THIS ROLE

AREAS TO GROW
_____

ROLE CALL

Role _____

WHAT I AM GRATEFUL FOR ABOUT THIS ROLE
_____

WHAT I ENJOYED MOST ABOUT THIS ROLE TODAY

WHAT I WANT TO DO MORE OF IN THIS ROLE

AREAS TO GROW
_____

Role _____

WHAT I AM GRATEFUL FOR ABOUT THIS ROLE
_____

WHAT I ENJOYED MOST ABOUT THIS ROLE TODAY

WHAT I WANT TO DO MORE OF IN THIS ROLE

AREAS TO GROW
_____

Role _____

WHAT I AM GRATEFUL FOR ABOUT THIS ROLE
_____

WHAT I ENJOYED MOST ABOUT THIS ROLE TODAY

WHAT I WANT TO DO MORE OF IN THIS ROLE

AREAS TO GROW
_____

Role _____

WHAT I AM GRATEFUL FOR ABOUT THIS ROLE
_____

WHAT I ENJOYED MOST ABOUT THIS ROLE TODAY

WHAT I WANT TO DO MORE OF IN THIS ROLE

AREAS TO GROW
_____

Role _____

WHAT I AM GRATEFUL FOR ABOUT THIS ROLE
_____

WHAT I ENJOYED MOST ABOUT THIS ROLE TODAY

WHAT I WANT TO DO MORE OF IN THIS ROLE

AREAS TO GROW
_____

Bedtime BRAIN DUMP

- ☐ _____
- ☐ _____
- ☐ _____
- ☐ _____
- ☐ _____
- ☐ _____
- ☐ _____
- ☐ _____
- ☐ _____
- ☐ _____
- ☐ _____
- ☐ _____
- ☐ _____
- ☐ _____
- ☐ _____

GAME PLAN FOR TOMORROW

_____
_____
_____
_____
_____
_____
_____
_____

I'M LOOKING FORWARD TO

_____
_____
_____
_____
_____
_____
_____
_____

ROLE CALL

Role _____

WHAT I AM GRATEFUL FOR ABOUT THIS ROLE
_____

WHAT I ENJOYED MOST ABOUT THIS ROLE TODAY

WHAT I WANT TO DO MORE OF IN THIS ROLE

AREAS TO GROW
_____

Role _____

WHAT I AM GRATEFUL FOR ABOUT THIS ROLE
_____

WHAT I ENJOYED MOST ABOUT THIS ROLE TODAY

WHAT I WANT TO DO MORE OF IN THIS ROLE

AREAS TO GROW
_____

Role _____

WHAT I AM GRATEFUL FOR ABOUT THIS ROLE
_____

WHAT I ENJOYED MOST ABOUT THIS ROLE TODAY

WHAT I WANT TO DO MORE OF IN THIS ROLE

AREAS TO GROW
_____

Role _____

WHAT I AM GRATEFUL FOR ABOUT THIS ROLE
_____

WHAT I ENJOYED MOST ABOUT THIS ROLE TODAY

WHAT I WANT TO DO MORE OF IN THIS ROLE

AREAS TO GROW
_____

Role _____

WHAT I AM GRATEFUL FOR ABOUT THIS ROLE
_____

WHAT I ENJOYED MOST ABOUT THIS ROLE TODAY

WHAT I WANT TO DO MORE OF IN THIS ROLE

AREAS TO GROW
_____

ROLE CALL

Role _____

WHAT I AM GRATEFUL FOR ABOUT THIS ROLE
_____

WHAT I ENJOYED MOST ABOUT THIS ROLE TODAY

WHAT I WANT TO DO MORE OF IN THIS ROLE

AREAS TO GROW
_____

Role _____

WHAT I AM GRATEFUL FOR ABOUT THIS ROLE
_____

WHAT I ENJOYED MOST ABOUT THIS ROLE TODAY

WHAT I WANT TO DO MORE OF IN THIS ROLE

AREAS TO GROW
_____

Role _____

WHAT I AM GRATEFUL FOR ABOUT THIS ROLE
_____

WHAT I ENJOYED MOST ABOUT THIS ROLE TODAY

WHAT I WANT TO DO MORE OF IN THIS ROLE

AREAS TO GROW
_____

Role _____

WHAT I AM GRATEFUL FOR ABOUT THIS ROLE
_____

WHAT I ENJOYED MOST ABOUT THIS ROLE TODAY

WHAT I WANT TO DO MORE OF IN THIS ROLE

AREAS TO GROW
_____

Role _____

WHAT I AM GRATEFUL FOR ABOUT THIS ROLE
_____

WHAT I ENJOYED MOST ABOUT THIS ROLE TODAY

WHAT I WANT TO DO MORE OF IN THIS ROLE

AREAS TO GROW
_____

Bedtime BRAIN DUMP

- [ ] _____
- [ ] _____
- [ ] _____
- [ ] _____
- [ ] _____
- [ ] _____
- [ ] _____
- [ ] _____
- [ ] _____
- [ ] _____
- [ ] _____
- [ ] _____
- [ ] _____
- [ ] _____

GAME PLAN FOR TOMORROW

I'M LOOKING FORWARD TO

ROLE CALL

Role _____

WHAT I AM GRATEFUL FOR ABOUT THIS ROLE
_____

WHAT I ENJOYED MOST ABOUT THIS ROLE TODAY

WHAT I WANT TO DO MORE OF IN THIS ROLE

AREAS TO GROW
_____

Role _____

WHAT I AM GRATEFUL FOR ABOUT THIS ROLE
_____

WHAT I ENJOYED MOST ABOUT THIS ROLE TODAY

WHAT I WANT TO DO MORE OF IN THIS ROLE

AREAS TO GROW
_____

Role _____

WHAT I AM GRATEFUL FOR ABOUT THIS ROLE
_____

WHAT I ENJOYED MOST ABOUT THIS ROLE TODAY

WHAT I WANT TO DO MORE OF IN THIS ROLE

AREAS TO GROW
_____

Role _____

WHAT I AM GRATEFUL FOR ABOUT THIS ROLE
_____

WHAT I ENJOYED MOST ABOUT THIS ROLE TODAY

WHAT I WANT TO DO MORE OF IN THIS ROLE

AREAS TO GROW
_____

Role _____

WHAT I AM GRATEFUL FOR ABOUT THIS ROLE
_____

WHAT I ENJOYED MOST ABOUT THIS ROLE TODAY

WHAT I WANT TO DO MORE OF IN THIS ROLE

AREAS TO GROW
_____

Bedtime BRAIN DUMP

GAME PLAN FOR TOMORROW

I'M LOOKING FORWARD TO

ROLE CALL

Role _____

WHAT I AM GRATEFUL FOR ABOUT THIS ROLE
_____

WHAT I ENJOYED MOST ABOUT THIS ROLE TODAY

WHAT I WANT TO DO MORE OF IN THIS ROLE

AREAS TO GROW
_____

Role _____

WHAT I AM GRATEFUL FOR ABOUT THIS ROLE
_____

WHAT I ENJOYED MOST ABOUT THIS ROLE TODAY

WHAT I WANT TO DO MORE OF IN THIS ROLE

AREAS TO GROW
_____

Role _____

WHAT I AM GRATEFUL FOR ABOUT THIS ROLE
_____

WHAT I ENJOYED MOST ABOUT THIS ROLE TODAY

WHAT I WANT TO DO MORE OF IN THIS ROLE

AREAS TO GROW
_____

Role _____

WHAT I AM GRATEFUL FOR ABOUT THIS ROLE
_____

WHAT I ENJOYED MOST ABOUT THIS ROLE TODAY

WHAT I WANT TO DO MORE OF IN THIS ROLE

AREAS TO GROW
_____

Role _____

WHAT I AM GRATEFUL FOR ABOUT THIS ROLE
_____

WHAT I ENJOYED MOST ABOUT THIS ROLE TODAY

WHAT I WANT TO DO MORE OF IN THIS ROLE

AREAS TO GROW
_____

Bedtime BRAIN DUMP

- [ ] _____
- [ ] _____
- [ ] _____
- [ ] _____
- [ ] _____
- [ ] _____
- [ ] _____
- [ ] _____
- [ ] _____
- [ ] _____
- [ ] _____
- [ ] _____
- [ ] _____
- [ ] _____

GAME PLAN FOR TOMORROW

_____
_____
_____
_____
_____
_____
_____
_____

I'M LOOKING FORWARD TO

_____
_____
_____
_____
_____
_____
_____
_____

ROLE CALL

Role _____
WHAT I AM GRATEFUL FOR ABOUT THIS ROLE
_____

WHAT I ENJOYED MOST ABOUT THIS ROLE TODAY

WHAT I WANT TO DO MORE OF IN THIS ROLE

AREAS TO GROW
_____

Role _____
WHAT I AM GRATEFUL FOR ABOUT THIS ROLE
_____

WHAT I ENJOYED MOST ABOUT THIS ROLE TODAY

WHAT I WANT TO DO MORE OF IN THIS ROLE

AREAS TO GROW
_____

Role _____
WHAT I AM GRATEFUL FOR ABOUT THIS ROLE
_____

WHAT I ENJOYED MOST ABOUT THIS ROLE TODAY

WHAT I WANT TO DO MORE OF IN THIS ROLE

AREAS TO GROW
_____

Role _____
WHAT I AM GRATEFUL FOR ABOUT THIS ROLE
_____

WHAT I ENJOYED MOST ABOUT THIS ROLE TODAY

WHAT I WANT TO DO MORE OF IN THIS ROLE

AREAS TO GROW
_____

Role _____
WHAT I AM GRATEFUL FOR ABOUT THIS ROLE
_____

WHAT I ENJOYED MOST ABOUT THIS ROLE TODAY

WHAT I WANT TO DO MORE OF IN THIS ROLE

AREAS TO GROW
_____

Bedtime BRAIN DUMP

- ☐ _____
- ☐ _____
- ☐ _____
- ☐ _____
- ☐ _____
- ☐ _____
- ☐ _____
- ☐ _____
- ☐ _____
- ☐ _____
- ☐ _____
- ☐ _____
- ☐ _____

GAME PLAN FOR TOMORROW

_____
_____
_____
_____
_____
_____
_____

I'M LOOKING FORWARD TO

_____
_____
_____
_____
_____
_____
_____

ROLE CALL

Role _____

WHAT I AM GRATEFUL FOR ABOUT THIS ROLE
_____

| WHAT I ENJOYED MOST ABOUT THIS ROLE TODAY | WHAT I WANT TO DO MORE OF IN THIS ROLE |

AREAS TO GROW
_____

Role _____

WHAT I AM GRATEFUL FOR ABOUT THIS ROLE
_____

| WHAT I ENJOYED MOST ABOUT THIS ROLE TODAY | WHAT I WANT TO DO MORE OF IN THIS ROLE |

AREAS TO GROW
_____

Role _____

WHAT I AM GRATEFUL FOR ABOUT THIS ROLE
_____

| WHAT I ENJOYED MOST ABOUT THIS ROLE TODAY | WHAT I WANT TO DO MORE OF IN THIS ROLE |

AREAS TO GROW
_____

Role _____

WHAT I AM GRATEFUL FOR ABOUT THIS ROLE
_____

| WHAT I ENJOYED MOST ABOUT THIS ROLE TODAY | WHAT I WANT TO DO MORE OF IN THIS ROLE |

AREAS TO GROW
_____

Role _____

WHAT I AM GRATEFUL FOR ABOUT THIS ROLE
_____

| WHAT I ENJOYED MOST ABOUT THIS ROLE TODAY | WHAT I WANT TO DO MORE OF IN THIS ROLE |

AREAS TO GROW
_____

Bedtime BRAIN DUMP

- _____
- _____
- _____
- _____
- _____
- _____
- _____
- _____
- _____
- _____
- _____
- _____
- _____
- _____

GAME PLAN FOR TOMORROW

_____
_____
_____
_____
_____
_____

I'M LOOKING FORWARD TO

_____
_____
_____
_____
_____
_____

ROLE CALL

Role _____

WHAT I AM GRATEFUL FOR ABOUT THIS ROLE
_____

WHAT I ENJOYED MOST ABOUT THIS ROLE TODAY

WHAT I WANT TO DO MORE OF IN THIS ROLE

AREAS TO GROW
_____

Role _____

WHAT I AM GRATEFUL FOR ABOUT THIS ROLE
_____

WHAT I ENJOYED MOST ABOUT THIS ROLE TODAY

WHAT I WANT TO DO MORE OF IN THIS ROLE

AREAS TO GROW
_____

Role _____

WHAT I AM GRATEFUL FOR ABOUT THIS ROLE
_____

WHAT I ENJOYED MOST ABOUT THIS ROLE TODAY

WHAT I WANT TO DO MORE OF IN THIS ROLE

AREAS TO GROW
_____

Role _____

WHAT I AM GRATEFUL FOR ABOUT THIS ROLE
_____

WHAT I ENJOYED MOST ABOUT THIS ROLE TODAY

WHAT I WANT TO DO MORE OF IN THIS ROLE

AREAS TO GROW
_____

Role _____

WHAT I AM GRATEFUL FOR ABOUT THIS ROLE
_____

WHAT I ENJOYED MOST ABOUT THIS ROLE TODAY

WHAT I WANT TO DO MORE OF IN THIS ROLE

AREAS TO GROW
_____

ROLE CALL

Role _____

WHAT I AM GRATEFUL FOR ABOUT THIS ROLE
_____

WHAT I ENJOYED MOST ABOUT THIS ROLE TODAY

WHAT I WANT TO DO MORE OF IN THIS ROLE

AREAS TO GROW
_____

Role _____

WHAT I AM GRATEFUL FOR ABOUT THIS ROLE
_____

WHAT I ENJOYED MOST ABOUT THIS ROLE TODAY

WHAT I WANT TO DO MORE OF IN THIS ROLE

AREAS TO GROW
_____

Role _____

WHAT I AM GRATEFUL FOR ABOUT THIS ROLE
_____

WHAT I ENJOYED MOST ABOUT THIS ROLE TODAY

WHAT I WANT TO DO MORE OF IN THIS ROLE

AREAS TO GROW
_____

Role _____

WHAT I AM GRATEFUL FOR ABOUT THIS ROLE
_____

WHAT I ENJOYED MOST ABOUT THIS ROLE TODAY

WHAT I WANT TO DO MORE OF IN THIS ROLE

AREAS TO GROW
_____

Role _____

WHAT I AM GRATEFUL FOR ABOUT THIS ROLE
_____

WHAT I ENJOYED MOST ABOUT THIS ROLE TODAY

WHAT I WANT TO DO MORE OF IN THIS ROLE

AREAS TO GROW
_____

Bedtime BRAIN DUMP

- ☐ _____
- ☐ _____
- ☐ _____
- ☐ _____
- ☐ _____
- ☐ _____
- ☐ _____
- ☐ _____
- ☐ _____
- ☐ _____
- ☐ _____
- ☐ _____
- ☐ _____
- ☐ _____

GAME PLAN FOR TOMORROW

_____
_____
_____
_____
_____
_____
_____

I'M LOOKING FORWARD TO

_____
_____
_____
_____
_____
_____
_____

ROLE CALL

Role _____

WHAT I AM GRATEFUL FOR ABOUT THIS ROLE
_____

WHAT I ENJOYED MOST ABOUT THIS ROLE TODAY

WHAT I WANT TO DO MORE OF IN THIS ROLE

AREAS TO GROW
_____

Role _____

WHAT I AM GRATEFUL FOR ABOUT THIS ROLE
_____

WHAT I ENJOYED MOST ABOUT THIS ROLE TODAY

WHAT I WANT TO DO MORE OF IN THIS ROLE

AREAS TO GROW
_____

Role _____

WHAT I AM GRATEFUL FOR ABOUT THIS ROLE
_____

WHAT I ENJOYED MOST ABOUT THIS ROLE TODAY

WHAT I WANT TO DO MORE OF IN THIS ROLE

AREAS TO GROW
_____

Role _____

WHAT I AM GRATEFUL FOR ABOUT THIS ROLE
_____

WHAT I ENJOYED MOST ABOUT THIS ROLE TODAY

WHAT I WANT TO DO MORE OF IN THIS ROLE

AREAS TO GROW
_____

Role _____

WHAT I AM GRATEFUL FOR ABOUT THIS ROLE
_____

WHAT I ENJOYED MOST ABOUT THIS ROLE TODAY

WHAT I WANT TO DO MORE OF IN THIS ROLE

AREAS TO GROW
_____

Bedtime BRAIN DUMP

☐ _____
☐ _____
☐ _____
☐ _____
☐ _____
☐ _____
☐ _____
☐ _____
☐ _____
☐ _____
☐ _____
☐ _____
☐ _____

GAME PLAN FOR TOMORROW

_____
_____
_____
_____
_____
_____
_____

I'M LOOKING FORWARD TO

_____
_____
_____
_____
_____
_____
_____

ROLE CALL

Role _____

WHAT I AM GRATEFUL FOR ABOUT THIS ROLE
_____

| WHAT I ENJOYED MOST ABOUT THIS ROLE TODAY | WHAT I WANT TO DO MORE OF IN THIS ROLE |

AREAS TO GROW
_____

Role _____

WHAT I AM GRATEFUL FOR ABOUT THIS ROLE
_____

| WHAT I ENJOYED MOST ABOUT THIS ROLE TODAY | WHAT I WANT TO DO MORE OF IN THIS ROLE |

AREAS TO GROW
_____

Role _____

WHAT I AM GRATEFUL FOR ABOUT THIS ROLE
_____

| WHAT I ENJOYED MOST ABOUT THIS ROLE TODAY | WHAT I WANT TO DO MORE OF IN THIS ROLE |

AREAS TO GROW
_____

Role _____

WHAT I AM GRATEFUL FOR ABOUT THIS ROLE
_____

| WHAT I ENJOYED MOST ABOUT THIS ROLE TODAY | WHAT I WANT TO DO MORE OF IN THIS ROLE |

AREAS TO GROW
_____

Role _____

WHAT I AM GRATEFUL FOR ABOUT THIS ROLE
_____

| WHAT I ENJOYED MOST ABOUT THIS ROLE TODAY | WHAT I WANT TO DO MORE OF IN THIS ROLE |

AREAS TO GROW
_____

Bedtime BRAIN DUMP

- _____
- _____
- _____
- _____
- _____
- _____
- _____
- _____
- _____
- _____
- _____
- _____
- _____
- _____

GAME PLAN FOR TOMORROW

_____
_____
_____
_____
_____
_____
_____

I'M LOOKING FORWARD TO

_____
_____
_____
_____
_____
_____
_____

ROLE CALL

Role _____

WHAT I AM GRATEFUL FOR ABOUT THIS ROLE
_____

WHAT I ENJOYED MOST ABOUT THIS ROLE TODAY

WHAT I WANT TO DO MORE OF IN THIS ROLE

AREAS TO GROW
_____

Role _____

WHAT I AM GRATEFUL FOR ABOUT THIS ROLE
_____

WHAT I ENJOYED MOST ABOUT THIS ROLE TODAY

WHAT I WANT TO DO MORE OF IN THIS ROLE

AREAS TO GROW
_____

Role _____

WHAT I AM GRATEFUL FOR ABOUT THIS ROLE
_____

WHAT I ENJOYED MOST ABOUT THIS ROLE TODAY

WHAT I WANT TO DO MORE OF IN THIS ROLE

AREAS TO GROW
_____

Role _____

WHAT I AM GRATEFUL FOR ABOUT THIS ROLE
_____

WHAT I ENJOYED MOST ABOUT THIS ROLE TODAY

WHAT I WANT TO DO MORE OF IN THIS ROLE

AREAS TO GROW
_____

Role _____

WHAT I AM GRATEFUL FOR ABOUT THIS ROLE
_____

WHAT I ENJOYED MOST ABOUT THIS ROLE TODAY

WHAT I WANT TO DO MORE OF IN THIS ROLE

AREAS TO GROW
_____

Bedtime BRAIN DUMP

- _____
- _____
- _____
- _____
- _____
- _____
- _____
- _____
- _____
- _____
- _____
- _____
- _____

GAME PLAN FOR TOMORROW

_____
_____
_____
_____
_____
_____
_____

I'M LOOKING FORWARD TO

_____
_____
_____
_____
_____
_____
_____

ROLE CALL

Role _____

WHAT I AM GRATEFUL FOR ABOUT THIS ROLE
_____

| WHAT I ENJOYED MOST ABOUT THIS ROLE TODAY | WHAT I WANT TO DO MORE OF IN THIS ROLE |

AREAS TO GROW
_____

Role _____

WHAT I AM GRATEFUL FOR ABOUT THIS ROLE
_____

| WHAT I ENJOYED MOST ABOUT THIS ROLE TODAY | WHAT I WANT TO DO MORE OF IN THIS ROLE |

AREAS TO GROW
_____

Role _____

WHAT I AM GRATEFUL FOR ABOUT THIS ROLE
_____

| WHAT I ENJOYED MOST ABOUT THIS ROLE TODAY | WHAT I WANT TO DO MORE OF IN THIS ROLE |

AREAS TO GROW
_____

Role _____

WHAT I AM GRATEFUL FOR ABOUT THIS ROLE
_____

| WHAT I ENJOYED MOST ABOUT THIS ROLE TODAY | WHAT I WANT TO DO MORE OF IN THIS ROLE |

AREAS TO GROW
_____

Role _____

WHAT I AM GRATEFUL FOR ABOUT THIS ROLE
_____

| WHAT I ENJOYED MOST ABOUT THIS ROLE TODAY | WHAT I WANT TO DO MORE OF IN THIS ROLE |

AREAS TO GROW
_____

Bedtime BRAIN DUMP

- [ ] _____
- [ ] _____
- [ ] _____
- [ ] _____
- [ ] _____
- [ ] _____
- [ ] _____
- [ ] _____
- [ ] _____
- [ ] _____
- [ ] _____
- [ ] _____
- [ ] _____

GAME PLAN FOR TOMORROW

_____
_____
_____
_____
_____
_____
_____

I'M LOOKING FORWARD TO

_____
_____
_____
_____
_____
_____
_____

ROLE CALL

Role _____

WHAT I AM GRATEFUL FOR ABOUT THIS ROLE
_____

WHAT I ENJOYED MOST ABOUT THIS ROLE TODAY

WHAT I WANT TO DO MORE OF IN THIS ROLE

AREAS TO GROW
_____

Role _____

WHAT I AM GRATEFUL FOR ABOUT THIS ROLE
_____

WHAT I ENJOYED MOST ABOUT THIS ROLE TODAY

WHAT I WANT TO DO MORE OF IN THIS ROLE

AREAS TO GROW
_____

Role _____

WHAT I AM GRATEFUL FOR ABOUT THIS ROLE
_____

WHAT I ENJOYED MOST ABOUT THIS ROLE TODAY

WHAT I WANT TO DO MORE OF IN THIS ROLE

AREAS TO GROW
_____

Role _____

WHAT I AM GRATEFUL FOR ABOUT THIS ROLE
_____

WHAT I ENJOYED MOST ABOUT THIS ROLE TODAY

WHAT I WANT TO DO MORE OF IN THIS ROLE

AREAS TO GROW
_____

Role _____

WHAT I AM GRATEFUL FOR ABOUT THIS ROLE
_____

WHAT I ENJOYED MOST ABOUT THIS ROLE TODAY

WHAT I WANT TO DO MORE OF IN THIS ROLE

AREAS TO GROW
_____

Bedtime BRAIN DUMP

- _____
- _____
- _____
- _____
- _____
- _____
- _____
- _____
- _____
- _____
- _____
- _____
- _____

GAME PLAN FOR TOMORROW

_____
_____
_____
_____
_____
_____
_____
_____

I'M LOOKING FORWARD TO

_____
_____
_____
_____
_____
_____
_____
_____

ROLE CALL

Role _____

WHAT I AM GRATEFUL FOR ABOUT THIS ROLE
_____

| WHAT I ENJOYED MOST ABOUT THIS ROLE TODAY | WHAT I WANT TO DO MORE OF IN THIS ROLE |

AREAS TO GROW
_____

Role _____

WHAT I AM GRATEFUL FOR ABOUT THIS ROLE
_____

| WHAT I ENJOYED MOST ABOUT THIS ROLE TODAY | WHAT I WANT TO DO MORE OF IN THIS ROLE |

AREAS TO GROW
_____

Role _____

WHAT I AM GRATEFUL FOR ABOUT THIS ROLE
_____

| WHAT I ENJOYED MOST ABOUT THIS ROLE TODAY | WHAT I WANT TO DO MORE OF IN THIS ROLE |

AREAS TO GROW
_____

Role _____

WHAT I AM GRATEFUL FOR ABOUT THIS ROLE
_____

| WHAT I ENJOYED MOST ABOUT THIS ROLE TODAY | WHAT I WANT TO DO MORE OF IN THIS ROLE |

AREAS TO GROW
_____

Role _____

WHAT I AM GRATEFUL FOR ABOUT THIS ROLE
_____

| WHAT I ENJOYED MOST ABOUT THIS ROLE TODAY | WHAT I WANT TO DO MORE OF IN THIS ROLE |

AREAS TO GROW
_____

Bedtime BRAIN DUMP

- _____
- _____
- _____
- _____
- _____
- _____
- _____
- _____
- _____
- _____
- _____
- _____
- _____
- _____

GAME PLAN FOR TOMORROW

_____
_____
_____
_____
_____
_____
_____

I'M LOOKING FORWARD TO

_____
_____
_____
_____
_____
_____
_____

ROLE CALL

Role _____
WHAT I AM GRATEFUL FOR ABOUT THIS ROLE

WHAT I ENJOYED MOST ABOUT THIS ROLE TODAY | WHAT I WANT TO DO MORE OF IN THIS ROLE

AREAS TO GROW

Role _____
WHAT I AM GRATEFUL FOR ABOUT THIS ROLE

WHAT I ENJOYED MOST ABOUT THIS ROLE TODAY | WHAT I WANT TO DO MORE OF IN THIS ROLE

AREAS TO GROW

Role _____
WHAT I AM GRATEFUL FOR ABOUT THIS ROLE

WHAT I ENJOYED MOST ABOUT THIS ROLE TODAY | WHAT I WANT TO DO MORE OF IN THIS ROLE

AREAS TO GROW

Role _____
WHAT I AM GRATEFUL FOR ABOUT THIS ROLE

WHAT I ENJOYED MOST ABOUT THIS ROLE TODAY | WHAT I WANT TO DO MORE OF IN THIS ROLE

AREAS TO GROW

Role _____
WHAT I AM GRATEFUL FOR ABOUT THIS ROLE

WHAT I ENJOYED MOST ABOUT THIS ROLE TODAY | WHAT I WANT TO DO MORE OF IN THIS ROLE

AREAS TO GROW

Bedtime BRAIN DUMP

GAME PLAN FOR TOMORROW

I'M LOOKING FORWARD TO

ROLE CALL

Role _____

WHAT I AM GRATEFUL FOR ABOUT THIS ROLE
_____

WHAT I ENJOYED MOST ABOUT THIS ROLE TODAY

WHAT I WANT TO DO MORE OF IN THIS ROLE

AREAS TO GROW
_____

Role _____

WHAT I AM GRATEFUL FOR ABOUT THIS ROLE
_____

WHAT I ENJOYED MOST ABOUT THIS ROLE TODAY

WHAT I WANT TO DO MORE OF IN THIS ROLE

AREAS TO GROW
_____

Role _____

WHAT I AM GRATEFUL FOR ABOUT THIS ROLE
_____

WHAT I ENJOYED MOST ABOUT THIS ROLE TODAY

WHAT I WANT TO DO MORE OF IN THIS ROLE

AREAS TO GROW
_____

Role _____

WHAT I AM GRATEFUL FOR ABOUT THIS ROLE
_____

WHAT I ENJOYED MOST ABOUT THIS ROLE TODAY

WHAT I WANT TO DO MORE OF IN THIS ROLE

AREAS TO GROW
_____

Role _____

WHAT I AM GRATEFUL FOR ABOUT THIS ROLE
_____

WHAT I ENJOYED MOST ABOUT THIS ROLE TODAY

WHAT I WANT TO DO MORE OF IN THIS ROLE

AREAS TO GROW
_____

Bedtime BRAIN DUMP

GAME PLAN FOR TOMORROW

I'M LOOKING FORWARD TO

in the bag!

ROLE CALL

Role _____   WHAT I AM GRATEFUL FOR ABOUT THIS ROLE
_____

WHAT I ENJOYED MOST ABOUT THIS ROLE TODAY | WHAT I WANT TO DO MORE OF IN THIS ROLE

AREAS TO GROW
_____

Role _____   WHAT I AM GRATEFUL FOR ABOUT THIS ROLE
_____

WHAT I ENJOYED MOST ABOUT THIS ROLE TODAY | WHAT I WANT TO DO MORE OF IN THIS ROLE

AREAS TO GROW
_____

Role _____   WHAT I AM GRATEFUL FOR ABOUT THIS ROLE
_____

WHAT I ENJOYED MOST ABOUT THIS ROLE TODAY | WHAT I WANT TO DO MORE OF IN THIS ROLE

AREAS TO GROW
_____

Role _____   WHAT I AM GRATEFUL FOR ABOUT THIS ROLE
_____

WHAT I ENJOYED MOST ABOUT THIS ROLE TODAY | WHAT I WANT TO DO MORE OF IN THIS ROLE

AREAS TO GROW
_____

Role _____   WHAT I AM GRATEFUL FOR ABOUT THIS ROLE
_____

WHAT I ENJOYED MOST ABOUT THIS ROLE TODAY | WHAT I WANT TO DO MORE OF IN THIS ROLE

AREAS TO GROW
_____

Bedtime BRAIN DUMP

- [ ] _____
- [ ] _____
- [ ] _____
- [ ] _____
- [ ] _____
- [ ] _____
- [ ] _____
- [ ] _____
- [ ] _____
- [ ] _____
- [ ] _____
- [ ] _____
- [ ] _____
- [ ] _____

GAME PLAN FOR TOMORROW

_____
_____
_____
_____
_____
_____
_____
_____

I'M LOOKING FORWARD TO

_____
_____
_____
_____
_____
_____
_____
_____

ROLE CALL

Role _____

WHAT I AM GRATEFUL FOR ABOUT THIS ROLE
_____

WHAT I ENJOYED MOST ABOUT THIS ROLE TODAY

WHAT I WANT TO DO MORE OF IN THIS ROLE

AREAS TO GROW
_____

Role _____

WHAT I AM GRATEFUL FOR ABOUT THIS ROLE
_____

WHAT I ENJOYED MOST ABOUT THIS ROLE TODAY

WHAT I WANT TO DO MORE OF IN THIS ROLE

AREAS TO GROW
_____

Role _____

WHAT I AM GRATEFUL FOR ABOUT THIS ROLE
_____

WHAT I ENJOYED MOST ABOUT THIS ROLE TODAY

WHAT I WANT TO DO MORE OF IN THIS ROLE

AREAS TO GROW
_____

Role _____

WHAT I AM GRATEFUL FOR ABOUT THIS ROLE
_____

WHAT I ENJOYED MOST ABOUT THIS ROLE TODAY

WHAT I WANT TO DO MORE OF IN THIS ROLE

AREAS TO GROW
_____

Role _____

WHAT I AM GRATEFUL FOR ABOUT THIS ROLE
_____

WHAT I ENJOYED MOST ABOUT THIS ROLE TODAY

WHAT I WANT TO DO MORE OF IN THIS ROLE

AREAS TO GROW
_____

Bedtime BRAIN DUMP

- ☐ _____
- ☐ _____
- ☐ _____
- ☐ _____
- ☐ _____
- ☐ _____
- ☐ _____
- ☐ _____
- ☐ _____
- ☐ _____
- ☐ _____
- ☐ _____
- ☐ _____
- ☐ _____

GAME PLAN FOR TOMORROW

_____
_____
_____
_____
_____
_____
_____
_____

I'M LOOKING FORWARD TO

_____
_____
_____
_____
_____
_____
_____
_____

ROLE CALL

Role _____

WHAT I AM GRATEFUL FOR ABOUT THIS ROLE
_____

WHAT I ENJOYED MOST ABOUT THIS ROLE TODAY

WHAT I WANT TO DO MORE OF IN THIS ROLE

AREAS TO GROW
_____

Role _____

WHAT I AM GRATEFUL FOR ABOUT THIS ROLE
_____

WHAT I ENJOYED MOST ABOUT THIS ROLE TODAY

WHAT I WANT TO DO MORE OF IN THIS ROLE

AREAS TO GROW
_____

Role _____

WHAT I AM GRATEFUL FOR ABOUT THIS ROLE
_____

WHAT I ENJOYED MOST ABOUT THIS ROLE TODAY

WHAT I WANT TO DO MORE OF IN THIS ROLE

AREAS TO GROW
_____

Role _____

WHAT I AM GRATEFUL FOR ABOUT THIS ROLE
_____

WHAT I ENJOYED MOST ABOUT THIS ROLE TODAY

WHAT I WANT TO DO MORE OF IN THIS ROLE

AREAS TO GROW
_____

Role _____

WHAT I AM GRATEFUL FOR ABOUT THIS ROLE
_____

WHAT I ENJOYED MOST ABOUT THIS ROLE TODAY

WHAT I WANT TO DO MORE OF IN THIS ROLE

AREAS TO GROW
_____

Bedtime BRAIN DUMP

- _____
- _____
- _____
- _____
- _____
- _____
- _____
- _____
- _____
- _____
- _____
- _____
- _____

GAME PLAN FOR TOMORROW

_____
_____
_____
_____
_____
_____
_____
_____

I'M LOOKING FORWARD TO

_____
_____
_____
_____
_____
_____
_____
_____

ROLE CALL

Role _____

WHAT I AM GRATEFUL FOR ABOUT THIS ROLE
_____

WHAT I ENJOYED MOST ABOUT THIS ROLE TODAY

WHAT I WANT TO DO MORE OF IN THIS ROLE

AREAS TO GROW
_____

Role _____

WHAT I AM GRATEFUL FOR ABOUT THIS ROLE
_____

WHAT I ENJOYED MOST ABOUT THIS ROLE TODAY

WHAT I WANT TO DO MORE OF IN THIS ROLE

AREAS TO GROW
_____

Role _____

WHAT I AM GRATEFUL FOR ABOUT THIS ROLE
_____

WHAT I ENJOYED MOST ABOUT THIS ROLE TODAY

WHAT I WANT TO DO MORE OF IN THIS ROLE

AREAS TO GROW
_____

Role _____

WHAT I AM GRATEFUL FOR ABOUT THIS ROLE
_____

WHAT I ENJOYED MOST ABOUT THIS ROLE TODAY

WHAT I WANT TO DO MORE OF IN THIS ROLE

AREAS TO GROW
_____

Role _____

WHAT I AM GRATEFUL FOR ABOUT THIS ROLE
_____

WHAT I ENJOYED MOST ABOUT THIS ROLE TODAY

WHAT I WANT TO DO MORE OF IN THIS ROLE

AREAS TO GROW
_____

Bedtime BRAIN DUMP

- [ ] _____
- [ ] _____
- [ ] _____
- [ ] _____
- [ ] _____
- [ ] _____
- [ ] _____
- [ ] _____
- [ ] _____
- [ ] _____
- [ ] _____
- [ ] _____
- [ ] _____
- [ ] _____

GAME PLAN FOR TOMORROW

_____
_____
_____
_____
_____
_____
_____

I'M LOOKING FORWARD TO

_____
_____
_____
_____
_____
_____
_____

ROLE CALL

Role _____

WHAT I AM GRATEFUL FOR ABOUT THIS ROLE
_____

WHAT I ENJOYED MOST ABOUT THIS ROLE TODAY

WHAT I WANT TO DO MORE OF IN THIS ROLE

AREAS TO GROW
_____

Role _____

WHAT I AM GRATEFUL FOR ABOUT THIS ROLE
_____

WHAT I ENJOYED MOST ABOUT THIS ROLE TODAY

WHAT I WANT TO DO MORE OF IN THIS ROLE

AREAS TO GROW
_____

Role _____

WHAT I AM GRATEFUL FOR ABOUT THIS ROLE
_____

WHAT I ENJOYED MOST ABOUT THIS ROLE TODAY

WHAT I WANT TO DO MORE OF IN THIS ROLE

AREAS TO GROW
_____

Role _____

WHAT I AM GRATEFUL FOR ABOUT THIS ROLE
_____

WHAT I ENJOYED MOST ABOUT THIS ROLE TODAY

WHAT I WANT TO DO MORE OF IN THIS ROLE

AREAS TO GROW
_____

Role _____

WHAT I AM GRATEFUL FOR ABOUT THIS ROLE
_____

WHAT I ENJOYED MOST ABOUT THIS ROLE TODAY

WHAT I WANT TO DO MORE OF IN THIS ROLE

AREAS TO GROW
_____

Bedtime BRAIN DUMP

- _____
- _____
- _____
- _____
- _____
- _____
- _____
- _____
- _____
- _____
- _____
- _____
- _____
- _____

GAME PLAN FOR TOMORROW

_____
_____
_____
_____
_____
_____
_____

I'M LOOKING FORWARD TO

_____
_____
_____
_____
_____
_____
_____

ROLE CALL

Role _____

WHAT I AM GRATEFUL FOR ABOUT THIS ROLE
_____

WHAT I ENJOYED MOST ABOUT THIS ROLE TODAY

WHAT I WANT TO DO MORE OF IN THIS ROLE

AREAS TO GROW
_____

Role _____

WHAT I AM GRATEFUL FOR ABOUT THIS ROLE
_____

WHAT I ENJOYED MOST ABOUT THIS ROLE TODAY

WHAT I WANT TO DO MORE OF IN THIS ROLE

AREAS TO GROW
_____

Role _____

WHAT I AM GRATEFUL FOR ABOUT THIS ROLE
_____

WHAT I ENJOYED MOST ABOUT THIS ROLE TODAY

WHAT I WANT TO DO MORE OF IN THIS ROLE

AREAS TO GROW
_____

Role _____

WHAT I AM GRATEFUL FOR ABOUT THIS ROLE
_____

WHAT I ENJOYED MOST ABOUT THIS ROLE TODAY

WHAT I WANT TO DO MORE OF IN THIS ROLE

AREAS TO GROW
_____

Role _____

WHAT I AM GRATEFUL FOR ABOUT THIS ROLE
_____

WHAT I ENJOYED MOST ABOUT THIS ROLE TODAY

WHAT I WANT TO DO MORE OF IN THIS ROLE

AREAS TO GROW
_____

Bedtime BRAIN DUMP

- ☐ _____
- ☐ _____
- ☐ _____
- ☐ _____
- ☐ _____
- ☐ _____
- ☐ _____
- ☐ _____
- ☐ _____
- ☐ _____
- ☐ _____
- ☐ _____
- ☐ _____
- ☐ _____

GAME PLAN FOR TOMORROW

_____
_____
_____
_____
_____
_____
_____
_____

I'M LOOKING FORWARD TO

_____
_____
_____
_____
_____
_____
_____
_____

ROLE CALL

Role _____

WHAT I AM GRATEFUL FOR ABOUT THIS ROLE
_____

WHAT I ENJOYED MOST ABOUT THIS ROLE TODAY

WHAT I WANT TO DO MORE OF IN THIS ROLE

AREAS TO GROW
_____

Role _____

WHAT I AM GRATEFUL FOR ABOUT THIS ROLE
_____

WHAT I ENJOYED MOST ABOUT THIS ROLE TODAY

WHAT I WANT TO DO MORE OF IN THIS ROLE

AREAS TO GROW
_____

Role _____

WHAT I AM GRATEFUL FOR ABOUT THIS ROLE
_____

WHAT I ENJOYED MOST ABOUT THIS ROLE TODAY

WHAT I WANT TO DO MORE OF IN THIS ROLE

AREAS TO GROW
_____

Role _____

WHAT I AM GRATEFUL FOR ABOUT THIS ROLE
_____

WHAT I ENJOYED MOST ABOUT THIS ROLE TODAY

WHAT I WANT TO DO MORE OF IN THIS ROLE

AREAS TO GROW
_____

Role _____

WHAT I AM GRATEFUL FOR ABOUT THIS ROLE
_____

WHAT I ENJOYED MOST ABOUT THIS ROLE TODAY

WHAT I WANT TO DO MORE OF IN THIS ROLE

AREAS TO GROW
_____

ROLE CALL

Role _____

WHAT I AM GRATEFUL FOR ABOUT THIS ROLE
_____

WHAT I ENJOYED MOST ABOUT THIS ROLE TODAY

WHAT I WANT TO DO MORE OF IN THIS ROLE

AREAS TO GROW
_____

Role _____

WHAT I AM GRATEFUL FOR ABOUT THIS ROLE
_____

WHAT I ENJOYED MOST ABOUT THIS ROLE TODAY

WHAT I WANT TO DO MORE OF IN THIS ROLE

AREAS TO GROW
_____

Role _____

WHAT I AM GRATEFUL FOR ABOUT THIS ROLE
_____

WHAT I ENJOYED MOST ABOUT THIS ROLE TODAY

WHAT I WANT TO DO MORE OF IN THIS ROLE

AREAS TO GROW
_____

Role _____

WHAT I AM GRATEFUL FOR ABOUT THIS ROLE
_____

WHAT I ENJOYED MOST ABOUT THIS ROLE TODAY

WHAT I WANT TO DO MORE OF IN THIS ROLE

AREAS TO GROW
_____

Role _____

WHAT I AM GRATEFUL FOR ABOUT THIS ROLE
_____

WHAT I ENJOYED MOST ABOUT THIS ROLE TODAY

WHAT I WANT TO DO MORE OF IN THIS ROLE

AREAS TO GROW
_____

Bedtime BRAIN DUMP

- _____
- _____
- _____
- _____
- _____
- _____
- _____
- _____
- _____
- _____
- _____
- _____
- _____
- _____

GAME PLAN FOR TOMORROW

_____

_____

_____

_____

_____

_____

_____

_____

I'M LOOKING FORWARD TO

_____

_____

_____

_____

_____

_____

_____

_____

ROLE CALL

Role _____   WHAT I AM GRATEFUL FOR ABOUT THIS ROLE
_____

| WHAT I ENJOYED MOST ABOUT THIS ROLE TODAY | WHAT I WANT TO DO MORE OF IN THIS ROLE |

AREAS TO GROW
_____

Role _____   WHAT I AM GRATEFUL FOR ABOUT THIS ROLE
_____

| WHAT I ENJOYED MOST ABOUT THIS ROLE TODAY | WHAT I WANT TO DO MORE OF IN THIS ROLE |

AREAS TO GROW
_____

Role _____   WHAT I AM GRATEFUL FOR ABOUT THIS ROLE
_____

| WHAT I ENJOYED MOST ABOUT THIS ROLE TODAY | WHAT I WANT TO DO MORE OF IN THIS ROLE |

AREAS TO GROW
_____

Role _____   WHAT I AM GRATEFUL FOR ABOUT THIS ROLE
_____

| WHAT I ENJOYED MOST ABOUT THIS ROLE TODAY | WHAT I WANT TO DO MORE OF IN THIS ROLE |

AREAS TO GROW
_____

Role _____   WHAT I AM GRATEFUL FOR ABOUT THIS ROLE
_____

| WHAT I ENJOYED MOST ABOUT THIS ROLE TODAY | WHAT I WANT TO DO MORE OF IN THIS ROLE |

AREAS TO GROW
_____

ROLE CALL

Role _____

WHAT I AM GRATEFUL FOR ABOUT THIS ROLE
_____

| WHAT I ENJOYED MOST ABOUT THIS ROLE TODAY | WHAT I WANT TO DO MORE OF IN THIS ROLE |

AREAS TO GROW
_____

Role _____

WHAT I AM GRATEFUL FOR ABOUT THIS ROLE
_____

| WHAT I ENJOYED MOST ABOUT THIS ROLE TODAY | WHAT I WANT TO DO MORE OF IN THIS ROLE |

AREAS TO GROW
_____

Role _____

WHAT I AM GRATEFUL FOR ABOUT THIS ROLE
_____

| WHAT I ENJOYED MOST ABOUT THIS ROLE TODAY | WHAT I WANT TO DO MORE OF IN THIS ROLE |

AREAS TO GROW
_____

Role _____

WHAT I AM GRATEFUL FOR ABOUT THIS ROLE
_____

| WHAT I ENJOYED MOST ABOUT THIS ROLE TODAY | WHAT I WANT TO DO MORE OF IN THIS ROLE |

AREAS TO GROW
_____

Role _____

WHAT I AM GRATEFUL FOR ABOUT THIS ROLE
_____

| WHAT I ENJOYED MOST ABOUT THIS ROLE TODAY | WHAT I WANT TO DO MORE OF IN THIS ROLE |

AREAS TO GROW
_____

Bedtime BRAIN DUMP

GAME PLAN FOR TOMORROW

I'M LOOKING FORWARD TO

ROLE CALL

Role _____   WHAT I AM GRATEFUL FOR ABOUT THIS ROLE
_____

| WHAT I ENJOYED MOST ABOUT THIS ROLE TODAY | WHAT I WANT TO DO MORE OF IN THIS ROLE |

AREAS TO GROW
_____

Role _____   WHAT I AM GRATEFUL FOR ABOUT THIS ROLE
_____

| WHAT I ENJOYED MOST ABOUT THIS ROLE TODAY | WHAT I WANT TO DO MORE OF IN THIS ROLE |

AREAS TO GROW
_____

Role _____   WHAT I AM GRATEFUL FOR ABOUT THIS ROLE
_____

| WHAT I ENJOYED MOST ABOUT THIS ROLE TODAY | WHAT I WANT TO DO MORE OF IN THIS ROLE |

AREAS TO GROW
_____

Role _____   WHAT I AM GRATEFUL FOR ABOUT THIS ROLE
_____

| WHAT I ENJOYED MOST ABOUT THIS ROLE TODAY | WHAT I WANT TO DO MORE OF IN THIS ROLE |

AREAS TO GROW
_____

Role _____   WHAT I AM GRATEFUL FOR ABOUT THIS ROLE
_____

| WHAT I ENJOYED MOST ABOUT THIS ROLE TODAY | WHAT I WANT TO DO MORE OF IN THIS ROLE |

AREAS TO GROW
_____

ROLE CALL

Role _____

WHAT I AM GRATEFUL FOR ABOUT THIS ROLE
_____

WHAT I ENJOYED MOST ABOUT THIS ROLE TODAY

WHAT I WANT TO DO MORE OF IN THIS ROLE

AREAS TO GROW
_____

Role _____

WHAT I AM GRATEFUL FOR ABOUT THIS ROLE
_____

WHAT I ENJOYED MOST ABOUT THIS ROLE TODAY

WHAT I WANT TO DO MORE OF IN THIS ROLE

AREAS TO GROW
_____

Role _____

WHAT I AM GRATEFUL FOR ABOUT THIS ROLE
_____

WHAT I ENJOYED MOST ABOUT THIS ROLE TODAY

WHAT I WANT TO DO MORE OF IN THIS ROLE

AREAS TO GROW
_____

Role _____

WHAT I AM GRATEFUL FOR ABOUT THIS ROLE
_____

WHAT I ENJOYED MOST ABOUT THIS ROLE TODAY

WHAT I WANT TO DO MORE OF IN THIS ROLE

AREAS TO GROW
_____

Role _____

WHAT I AM GRATEFUL FOR ABOUT THIS ROLE
_____

WHAT I ENJOYED MOST ABOUT THIS ROLE TODAY

WHAT I WANT TO DO MORE OF IN THIS ROLE

AREAS TO GROW
_____

Bedtime BRAIN DUMP

- ☐ _____
- ☐ _____
- ☐ _____
- ☐ _____
- ☐ _____
- ☐ _____
- ☐ _____
- ☐ _____
- ☐ _____
- ☐ _____
- ☐ _____
- ☐ _____
- ☐ _____

GAME PLAN FOR TOMORROW

_____
_____
_____
_____
_____
_____
_____
_____

I'M LOOKING FORWARD TO

_____
_____
_____
_____
_____
_____
_____
_____

ROLE CALL

Role _____

WHAT I AM GRATEFUL FOR ABOUT THIS ROLE
_____

WHAT I ENJOYED MOST ABOUT THIS ROLE TODAY

WHAT I WANT TO DO MORE OF IN THIS ROLE

AREAS TO GROW
_____

Role _____

WHAT I AM GRATEFUL FOR ABOUT THIS ROLE
_____

WHAT I ENJOYED MOST ABOUT THIS ROLE TODAY

WHAT I WANT TO DO MORE OF IN THIS ROLE

AREAS TO GROW
_____

Role _____

WHAT I AM GRATEFUL FOR ABOUT THIS ROLE
_____

WHAT I ENJOYED MOST ABOUT THIS ROLE TODAY

WHAT I WANT TO DO MORE OF IN THIS ROLE

AREAS TO GROW
_____

Role _____

WHAT I AM GRATEFUL FOR ABOUT THIS ROLE
_____

WHAT I ENJOYED MOST ABOUT THIS ROLE TODAY

WHAT I WANT TO DO MORE OF IN THIS ROLE

AREAS TO GROW
_____

Role _____

WHAT I AM GRATEFUL FOR ABOUT THIS ROLE
_____

WHAT I ENJOYED MOST ABOUT THIS ROLE TODAY

WHAT I WANT TO DO MORE OF IN THIS ROLE

AREAS TO GROW
_____

ROLE CALL

Role _____

WHAT I AM GRATEFUL FOR ABOUT THIS ROLE
_____

WHAT I ENJOYED MOST ABOUT THIS ROLE TODAY

WHAT I WANT TO DO MORE OF IN THIS ROLE

AREAS TO GROW
_____

Role _____

WHAT I AM GRATEFUL FOR ABOUT THIS ROLE
_____

WHAT I ENJOYED MOST ABOUT THIS ROLE TODAY

WHAT I WANT TO DO MORE OF IN THIS ROLE

AREAS TO GROW
_____

Role _____

WHAT I AM GRATEFUL FOR ABOUT THIS ROLE
_____

WHAT I ENJOYED MOST ABOUT THIS ROLE TODAY

WHAT I WANT TO DO MORE OF IN THIS ROLE

AREAS TO GROW
_____

Role _____

WHAT I AM GRATEFUL FOR ABOUT THIS ROLE
_____

WHAT I ENJOYED MOST ABOUT THIS ROLE TODAY

WHAT I WANT TO DO MORE OF IN THIS ROLE

AREAS TO GROW
_____

Role _____

WHAT I AM GRATEFUL FOR ABOUT THIS ROLE
_____

WHAT I ENJOYED MOST ABOUT THIS ROLE TODAY

WHAT I WANT TO DO MORE OF IN THIS ROLE

AREAS TO GROW
_____

Bedtime BRAIN DUMP

GAME PLAN FOR TOMORROW

I'M LOOKING FORWARD TO

ROLE CALL

Role _____ WHAT I AM GRATEFUL FOR ABOUT THIS ROLE
_____

| WHAT I ENJOYED MOST ABOUT THIS ROLE TODAY | WHAT I WANT TO DO MORE OF IN THIS ROLE |

AREAS TO GROW
_____

Role _____ WHAT I AM GRATEFUL FOR ABOUT THIS ROLE
_____

| WHAT I ENJOYED MOST ABOUT THIS ROLE TODAY | WHAT I WANT TO DO MORE OF IN THIS ROLE |

AREAS TO GROW
_____

Role _____ WHAT I AM GRATEFUL FOR ABOUT THIS ROLE
_____

| WHAT I ENJOYED MOST ABOUT THIS ROLE TODAY | WHAT I WANT TO DO MORE OF IN THIS ROLE |

AREAS TO GROW
_____

Role _____ WHAT I AM GRATEFUL FOR ABOUT THIS ROLE
_____

| WHAT I ENJOYED MOST ABOUT THIS ROLE TODAY | WHAT I WANT TO DO MORE OF IN THIS ROLE |

AREAS TO GROW
_____

Role _____ WHAT I AM GRATEFUL FOR ABOUT THIS ROLE
_____

| WHAT I ENJOYED MOST ABOUT THIS ROLE TODAY | WHAT I WANT TO DO MORE OF IN THIS ROLE |

AREAS TO GROW
_____

Bedtime BRAIN DUMP

GAME PLAN FOR TOMORROW

I'M LOOKING FORWARD TO

ROLE CALL

Role _____

WHAT I AM GRATEFUL FOR ABOUT THIS ROLE
_____

WHAT I ENJOYED MOST ABOUT THIS ROLE TODAY | WHAT I WANT TO DO MORE OF IN THIS ROLE

AREAS TO GROW
_____

Role _____

WHAT I AM GRATEFUL FOR ABOUT THIS ROLE
_____

WHAT I ENJOYED MOST ABOUT THIS ROLE TODAY | WHAT I WANT TO DO MORE OF IN THIS ROLE

AREAS TO GROW
_____

Role _____

WHAT I AM GRATEFUL FOR ABOUT THIS ROLE
_____

WHAT I ENJOYED MOST ABOUT THIS ROLE TODAY | WHAT I WANT TO DO MORE OF IN THIS ROLE

AREAS TO GROW
_____

Role _____

WHAT I AM GRATEFUL FOR ABOUT THIS ROLE
_____

WHAT I ENJOYED MOST ABOUT THIS ROLE TODAY | WHAT I WANT TO DO MORE OF IN THIS ROLE

AREAS TO GROW
_____

Role _____

WHAT I AM GRATEFUL FOR ABOUT THIS ROLE
_____

WHAT I ENJOYED MOST ABOUT THIS ROLE TODAY | WHAT I WANT TO DO MORE OF IN THIS ROLE

AREAS TO GROW
_____

Bedtime BRAIN DUMP

GAME PLAN FOR TOMORROW

I'M LOOKING FORWARD TO

ROLE CALL

Role _____   WHAT I AM GRATEFUL FOR ABOUT THIS ROLE
_____

| WHAT I ENJOYED MOST ABOUT THIS ROLE TODAY | WHAT I WANT TO DO MORE OF IN THIS ROLE |

AREAS TO GROW
_____

Role _____   WHAT I AM GRATEFUL FOR ABOUT THIS ROLE
_____

| WHAT I ENJOYED MOST ABOUT THIS ROLE TODAY | WHAT I WANT TO DO MORE OF IN THIS ROLE |

AREAS TO GROW
_____

Role _____   WHAT I AM GRATEFUL FOR ABOUT THIS ROLE
_____

| WHAT I ENJOYED MOST ABOUT THIS ROLE TODAY | WHAT I WANT TO DO MORE OF IN THIS ROLE |

AREAS TO GROW
_____

Role _____   WHAT I AM GRATEFUL FOR ABOUT THIS ROLE
_____

| WHAT I ENJOYED MOST ABOUT THIS ROLE TODAY | WHAT I WANT TO DO MORE OF IN THIS ROLE |

AREAS TO GROW
_____

Role _____   WHAT I AM GRATEFUL FOR ABOUT THIS ROLE
_____

| WHAT I ENJOYED MOST ABOUT THIS ROLE TODAY | WHAT I WANT TO DO MORE OF IN THIS ROLE |

AREAS TO GROW
_____

Bedtime BRAIN DUMP

GAME PLAN FOR TOMORROW

I'M LOOKING FORWARD TO

ROLE CALL

Role _____

WHAT I AM GRATEFUL FOR ABOUT THIS ROLE
_____

WHAT I ENJOYED MOST ABOUT THIS ROLE TODAY

WHAT I WANT TO DO MORE OF IN THIS ROLE

AREAS TO GROW
_____

Role _____

WHAT I AM GRATEFUL FOR ABOUT THIS ROLE
_____

WHAT I ENJOYED MOST ABOUT THIS ROLE TODAY

WHAT I WANT TO DO MORE OF IN THIS ROLE

AREAS TO GROW
_____

Role _____

WHAT I AM GRATEFUL FOR ABOUT THIS ROLE
_____

WHAT I ENJOYED MOST ABOUT THIS ROLE TODAY

WHAT I WANT TO DO MORE OF IN THIS ROLE

AREAS TO GROW
_____

Role _____

WHAT I AM GRATEFUL FOR ABOUT THIS ROLE
_____

WHAT I ENJOYED MOST ABOUT THIS ROLE TODAY

WHAT I WANT TO DO MORE OF IN THIS ROLE

AREAS TO GROW
_____

Role _____

WHAT I AM GRATEFUL FOR ABOUT THIS ROLE
_____

WHAT I ENJOYED MOST ABOUT THIS ROLE TODAY

WHAT I WANT TO DO MORE OF IN THIS ROLE

AREAS TO GROW
_____

Bedtime BRAIN DUMP

GAME PLAN FOR TOMORROW

I'M LOOKING FORWARD TO

ROLE CALL

Role _____ WHAT I AM GRATEFUL FOR ABOUT THIS ROLE
_____

WHAT I ENJOYED MOST ABOUT THIS ROLE TODAY | WHAT I WANT TO DO MORE OF IN THIS ROLE

AREAS TO GROW
_____

Role _____ WHAT I AM GRATEFUL FOR ABOUT THIS ROLE
_____

WHAT I ENJOYED MOST ABOUT THIS ROLE TODAY | WHAT I WANT TO DO MORE OF IN THIS ROLE

AREAS TO GROW
_____

Role _____ WHAT I AM GRATEFUL FOR ABOUT THIS ROLE
_____

WHAT I ENJOYED MOST ABOUT THIS ROLE TODAY | WHAT I WANT TO DO MORE OF IN THIS ROLE

AREAS TO GROW
_____

Role _____ WHAT I AM GRATEFUL FOR ABOUT THIS ROLE
_____

WHAT I ENJOYED MOST ABOUT THIS ROLE TODAY | WHAT I WANT TO DO MORE OF IN THIS ROLE

AREAS TO GROW
_____

Role _____ WHAT I AM GRATEFUL FOR ABOUT THIS ROLE
_____

WHAT I ENJOYED MOST ABOUT THIS ROLE TODAY | WHAT I WANT TO DO MORE OF IN THIS ROLE

AREAS TO GROW
_____

ROLE CALL

Role _____ WHAT I AM GRATEFUL FOR ABOUT THIS ROLE
_____

WHAT I ENJOYED MOST ABOUT THIS ROLE TODAY | WHAT I WANT TO DO MORE OF IN THIS ROLE

AREAS TO GROW
_____

Role _____ WHAT I AM GRATEFUL FOR ABOUT THIS ROLE
_____

WHAT I ENJOYED MOST ABOUT THIS ROLE TODAY | WHAT I WANT TO DO MORE OF IN THIS ROLE

AREAS TO GROW
_____

Role _____ WHAT I AM GRATEFUL FOR ABOUT THIS ROLE
_____

WHAT I ENJOYED MOST ABOUT THIS ROLE TODAY | WHAT I WANT TO DO MORE OF IN THIS ROLE

AREAS TO GROW
_____

Role _____ WHAT I AM GRATEFUL FOR ABOUT THIS ROLE
_____

WHAT I ENJOYED MOST ABOUT THIS ROLE TODAY | WHAT I WANT TO DO MORE OF IN THIS ROLE

AREAS TO GROW
_____

Role _____ WHAT I AM GRATEFUL FOR ABOUT THIS ROLE
_____

WHAT I ENJOYED MOST ABOUT THIS ROLE TODAY | WHAT I WANT TO DO MORE OF IN THIS ROLE

AREAS TO GROW
_____

Bedtime BRAIN DUMP

GAME PLAN FOR TOMORROW

I'M LOOKING FORWARD TO

ROLE CALL

Role _____

WHAT I AM GRATEFUL FOR ABOUT THIS ROLE
_____

WHAT I ENJOYED MOST ABOUT THIS ROLE TODAY

WHAT I WANT TO DO MORE OF IN THIS ROLE

AREAS TO GROW
_____

Role _____

WHAT I AM GRATEFUL FOR ABOUT THIS ROLE
_____

WHAT I ENJOYED MOST ABOUT THIS ROLE TODAY

WHAT I WANT TO DO MORE OF IN THIS ROLE

AREAS TO GROW
_____

Role _____

WHAT I AM GRATEFUL FOR ABOUT THIS ROLE
_____

WHAT I ENJOYED MOST ABOUT THIS ROLE TODAY

WHAT I WANT TO DO MORE OF IN THIS ROLE

AREAS TO GROW
_____

Role _____

WHAT I AM GRATEFUL FOR ABOUT THIS ROLE
_____

WHAT I ENJOYED MOST ABOUT THIS ROLE TODAY

WHAT I WANT TO DO MORE OF IN THIS ROLE

AREAS TO GROW
_____

Role _____

WHAT I AM GRATEFUL FOR ABOUT THIS ROLE
_____

WHAT I ENJOYED MOST ABOUT THIS ROLE TODAY

WHAT I WANT TO DO MORE OF IN THIS ROLE

AREAS TO GROW
_____

Bedtime BRAIN DUMP

GAME PLAN FOR TOMORROW

I'M LOOKING FORWARD TO

ROLE CALL

Role _____

WHAT I AM GRATEFUL FOR ABOUT THIS ROLE
_____

WHAT I ENJOYED MOST ABOUT THIS ROLE TODAY

WHAT I WANT TO DO MORE OF IN THIS ROLE

AREAS TO GROW
_____

Role _____

WHAT I AM GRATEFUL FOR ABOUT THIS ROLE
_____

WHAT I ENJOYED MOST ABOUT THIS ROLE TODAY

WHAT I WANT TO DO MORE OF IN THIS ROLE

AREAS TO GROW
_____

Role _____

WHAT I AM GRATEFUL FOR ABOUT THIS ROLE
_____

WHAT I ENJOYED MOST ABOUT THIS ROLE TODAY

WHAT I WANT TO DO MORE OF IN THIS ROLE

AREAS TO GROW
_____

Role _____

WHAT I AM GRATEFUL FOR ABOUT THIS ROLE
_____

WHAT I ENJOYED MOST ABOUT THIS ROLE TODAY

WHAT I WANT TO DO MORE OF IN THIS ROLE

AREAS TO GROW
_____

Role _____

WHAT I AM GRATEFUL FOR ABOUT THIS ROLE
_____

WHAT I ENJOYED MOST ABOUT THIS ROLE TODAY

WHAT I WANT TO DO MORE OF IN THIS ROLE

AREAS TO GROW
_____

Bedtime BRAIN DUMP

GAME PLAN FOR TOMORROW

I'M LOOKING FORWARD TO

ROLE CALL

Role _____   WHAT I AM GRATEFUL FOR ABOUT THIS ROLE
_____

| WHAT I ENJOYED MOST ABOUT THIS ROLE TODAY | WHAT I WANT TO DO MORE OF IN THIS ROLE |

AREAS TO GROW
_____

Role _____   WHAT I AM GRATEFUL FOR ABOUT THIS ROLE
_____

| WHAT I ENJOYED MOST ABOUT THIS ROLE TODAY | WHAT I WANT TO DO MORE OF IN THIS ROLE |

AREAS TO GROW
_____

Role _____   WHAT I AM GRATEFUL FOR ABOUT THIS ROLE
_____

| WHAT I ENJOYED MOST ABOUT THIS ROLE TODAY | WHAT I WANT TO DO MORE OF IN THIS ROLE |

AREAS TO GROW
_____

Role _____   WHAT I AM GRATEFUL FOR ABOUT THIS ROLE
_____

| WHAT I ENJOYED MOST ABOUT THIS ROLE TODAY | WHAT I WANT TO DO MORE OF IN THIS ROLE |

AREAS TO GROW
_____

Role _____   WHAT I AM GRATEFUL FOR ABOUT THIS ROLE
_____

| WHAT I ENJOYED MOST ABOUT THIS ROLE TODAY | WHAT I WANT TO DO MORE OF IN THIS ROLE |

AREAS TO GROW
_____

Bedtime BRAIN DUMP

GAME PLAN FOR TOMORROW

I'M LOOKING FORWARD TO

ROLE CALL

Role _____   WHAT I AM GRATEFUL FOR ABOUT THIS ROLE
_____

WHAT I ENJOYED MOST ABOUT THIS ROLE TODAY | WHAT I WANT TO DO MORE OF IN THIS ROLE

AREAS TO GROW
_____

Role _____   WHAT I AM GRATEFUL FOR ABOUT THIS ROLE
_____

WHAT I ENJOYED MOST ABOUT THIS ROLE TODAY | WHAT I WANT TO DO MORE OF IN THIS ROLE

AREAS TO GROW
_____

Role _____   WHAT I AM GRATEFUL FOR ABOUT THIS ROLE
_____

WHAT I ENJOYED MOST ABOUT THIS ROLE TODAY | WHAT I WANT TO DO MORE OF IN THIS ROLE

AREAS TO GROW
_____

Role _____   WHAT I AM GRATEFUL FOR ABOUT THIS ROLE
_____

WHAT I ENJOYED MOST ABOUT THIS ROLE TODAY | WHAT I WANT TO DO MORE OF IN THIS ROLE

ARFAS TO GROW
_____

Role _____   WHAT I AM GRATEFUL FOR ABOUT THIS ROLE
_____

WHAT I ENJOYED MOST ABOUT THIS ROLE TODAY | WHAT I WANT TO DO MORE OF IN THIS ROLE

AREAS TO GROW
_____

Bedtime BRAIN DUMP

GAME PLAN FOR TOMORROW

I'M LOOKING FORWARD TO

ROLE CALL

Role _____

WHAT I AM GRATEFUL FOR ABOUT THIS ROLE
_____

WHAT I ENJOYED MOST ABOUT THIS ROLE TODAY

WHAT I WANT TO DO MORE OF IN THIS ROLE

AREAS TO GROW
_____

Role _____

WHAT I AM GRATEFUL FOR ABOUT THIS ROLE
_____

WHAT I ENJOYED MOST ABOUT THIS ROLE TODAY

WHAT I WANT TO DO MORE OF IN THIS ROLE

AREAS TO GROW
_____

Role _____

WHAT I AM GRATEFUL FOR ABOUT THIS ROLE
_____

WHAT I ENJOYED MOST ABOUT THIS ROLE TODAY

WHAT I WANT TO DO MORE OF IN THIS ROLE

AREAS TO GROW
_____

Role _____

WHAT I AM GRATEFUL FOR ABOUT THIS ROLE
_____

WHAT I ENJOYED MOST ABOUT THIS ROLE TODAY

WHAT I WANT TO DO MORE OF IN THIS ROLE

AREAS TO GROW
_____

Role _____

WHAT I AM GRATEFUL FOR ABOUT THIS ROLE
_____

WHAT I ENJOYED MOST ABOUT THIS ROLE TODAY

WHAT I WANT TO DO MORE OF IN THIS ROLE

AREAS TO GROW
_____

Bedtime BRAIN DUMP

- [ ] _____
- [ ] _____
- [ ] _____
- [ ] _____
- [ ] _____
- [ ] _____
- [ ] _____
- [ ] _____
- [ ] _____
- [ ] _____
- [ ] _____
- [ ] _____
- [ ] _____

GAME PLAN FOR TOMORROW

_____
_____
_____
_____
_____
_____
_____

I'M LOOKING FORWARD TO

_____
_____
_____
_____
_____
_____
_____

ROLE CALL

Role _____ WHAT I AM GRATEFUL FOR ABOUT THIS ROLE
_____

| WHAT I ENJOYED MOST ABOUT THIS ROLE TODAY | WHAT I WANT TO DO MORE OF IN THIS ROLE |

AREAS TO GROW
_____

Role _____ WHAT I AM GRATEFUL FOR ABOUT THIS ROLE
_____

| WHAT I ENJOYED MOST ABOUT THIS ROLE TODAY | WHAT I WANT TO DO MORE OF IN THIS ROLE |

AREAS TO GROW
_____

Role _____ WHAT I AM GRATEFUL FOR ABOUT THIS ROLE
_____

| WHAT I ENJOYED MOST ABOUT THIS ROLE TODAY | WHAT I WANT TO DO MORE OF IN THIS ROLE |

AREAS TO GROW
_____

Role _____ WHAT I AM GRATEFUL FOR ABOUT THIS ROLE
_____

| WHAT I ENJOYED MOST ABOUT THIS ROLE TODAY | WHAT I WANT TO DO MORE OF IN THIS ROLE |

AREAS TO GROW
_____

Role _____ WHAT I AM GRATEFUL FOR ABOUT THIS ROLE
_____

| WHAT I ENJOYED MOST ABOUT THIS ROLE TODAY | WHAT I WANT TO DO MORE OF IN THIS ROLE |

AREAS TO GROW
_____

Bedtime BRAIN DUMP

☐ _____
☐ _____
☐ _____
☐ _____
☐ _____
☐ _____
☐ _____
☐ _____
☐ _____
☐ _____
☐ _____
☐ _____

GAME PLAN FOR TOMORROW

_____
_____
_____
_____
_____
_____
_____

I'M LOOKING FORWARD TO

_____
_____
_____
_____
_____
_____
_____

ROLE CALL

Role _____

WHAT I AM GRATEFUL FOR ABOUT THIS ROLE
_____

WHAT I ENJOYED MOST ABOUT THIS ROLE TODAY | WHAT I WANT TO DO MORE OF IN THIS ROLE

AREAS TO GROW
_____

Role _____

WHAT I AM GRATEFUL FOR ABOUT THIS ROLE
_____

WHAT I ENJOYED MOST ABOUT THIS ROLE TODAY | WHAT I WANT TO DO MORE OF IN THIS ROLE

AREAS TO GROW
_____

Role _____

WHAT I AM GRATEFUL FOR ABOUT THIS ROLE
_____

WHAT I ENJOYED MOST ABOUT THIS ROLE TODAY | WHAT I WANT TO DO MORE OF IN THIS ROLE

AREAS TO GROW
_____

Role _____

WHAT I AM GRATEFUL FOR ABOUT THIS ROLE
_____

WHAT I ENJOYED MOST ABOUT THIS ROLE TODAY | WHAT I WANT TO DO MORE OF IN THIS ROLE

AREAS TO GROW
_____

Role _____

WHAT I AM GRATEFUL FOR ABOUT THIS ROLE
_____

WHAT I ENJOYED MOST ABOUT THIS ROLE TODAY | WHAT I WANT TO DO MORE OF IN THIS ROLE

AREAS TO GROW
_____

Bedtime BRAIN DUMP

- [ ] _____
- [ ] _____
- [ ] _____
- [ ] _____
- [ ] _____
- [ ] _____
- [ ] _____
- [ ] _____
- [ ] _____
- [ ] _____
- [ ] _____
- [ ] _____

GAME PLAN FOR TOMORROW

_____
_____
_____
_____
_____
_____
_____
_____

I'M LOOKING FORWARD TO

_____
_____
_____
_____
_____
_____
_____

ROLE CALL

Role _____

WHAT I AM GRATEFUL FOR ABOUT THIS ROLE
_____

WHAT I ENJOYED MOST ABOUT THIS ROLE TODAY | WHAT I WANT TO DO MORE OF IN THIS ROLE

AREAS TO GROW
_____

Role _____

WHAT I AM GRATEFUL FOR ABOUT THIS ROLE
_____

WHAT I ENJOYED MOST ABOUT THIS ROLE TODAY | WHAT I WANT TO DO MORE OF IN THIS ROLE

AREAS TO GROW
_____

Role _____

WHAT I AM GRATEFUL FOR ABOUT THIS ROLE
_____

WHAT I ENJOYED MOST ABOUT THIS ROLE TODAY | WHAT I WANT TO DO MORE OF IN THIS ROLE

AREAS TO GROW
_____

Role _____

WHAT I AM GRATEFUL FOR ABOUT THIS ROLE
_____

WHAT I ENJOYED MOST ABOUT THIS ROLE TODAY | WHAT I WANT TO DO MORE OF IN THIS ROLE

AREAS TO GROW
_____

Role _____

WHAT I AM GRATEFUL FOR ABOUT THIS ROLE
_____

WHAT I ENJOYED MOST ABOUT THIS ROLE TODAY | WHAT I WANT TO DO MORE OF IN THIS ROLE

AREAS TO GROW
_____

Bedtime BRAIN DUMP

GAME PLAN FOR TOMORROW

I'M LOOKING FORWARD TO

ROLE CALL

Role _____

WHAT I AM GRATEFUL FOR ABOUT THIS ROLE
_____

WHAT I ENJOYED MOST ABOUT THIS ROLE TODAY

WHAT I WANT TO DO MORE OF IN THIS ROLE

AREAS TO GROW
_____

Role _____

WHAT I AM GRATEFUL FOR ABOUT THIS ROLE
_____

WHAT I ENJOYED MOST ABOUT THIS ROLE TODAY

WHAT I WANT TO DO MORE OF IN THIS ROLE

AREAS TO GROW
_____

Role _____

WHAT I AM GRATEFUL FOR ABOUT THIS ROLE
_____

WHAT I ENJOYED MOST ABOUT THIS ROLE TODAY

WHAT I WANT TO DO MORE OF IN THIS ROLE

AREAS TO GROW
_____

Role _____

WHAT I AM GRATEFUL FOR ABOUT THIS ROLE
_____

WHAT I ENJOYED MOST ABOUT THIS ROLE TODAY

WHAT I WANT TO DO MORE OF IN THIS ROLE

AREAS TO GROW
_____

Role _____

WHAT I AM GRATEFUL FOR ABOUT THIS ROLE
_____

WHAT I ENJOYED MOST ABOUT THIS ROLE TODAY

WHAT I WANT TO DO MORE OF IN THIS ROLE

AREAS TO GROW
_____

Bedtime BRAIN DUMP

- [ ] _____
- [ ] _____
- [ ] _____
- [ ] _____
- [ ] _____
- [ ] _____
- [ ] _____
- [ ] _____
- [ ] _____
- [ ] _____
- [ ] _____
- [ ] _____
- [ ] _____
- [ ] _____

GAME PLAN FOR TOMORROW

_____
_____
_____
_____
_____
_____
_____
_____

I'M LOOKING FORWARD TO

_____
_____
_____
_____
_____
_____
_____
_____

ROLE CALL

Role _____

WHAT I AM GRATEFUL FOR ABOUT THIS ROLE
_____

| WHAT I ENJOYED MOST ABOUT THIS ROLE TODAY | WHAT I WANT TO DO MORE OF IN THIS ROLE |

AREAS TO GROW
_____

Role _____

WHAT I AM GRATEFUL FOR ABOUT THIS ROLE
_____

| WHAT I ENJOYED MOST ABOUT THIS ROLE TODAY | WHAT I WANT TO DO MORE OF IN THIS ROLE |

AREAS TO GROW
_____

Role _____

WHAT I AM GRATEFUL FOR ABOUT THIS ROLE
_____

| WHAT I ENJOYED MOST ABOUT THIS ROLE TODAY | WHAT I WANT TO DO MORE OF IN THIS ROLE |

AREAS TO GROW
_____

Role _____

WHAT I AM GRATEFUL FOR ABOUT THIS ROLE
_____

| WHAT I ENJOYED MOST ABOUT THIS ROLE TODAY | WHAT I WANT TO DO MORE OF IN THIS ROLE |

AREAS TO GROW
_____

Role _____

WHAT I AM GRATEFUL FOR ABOUT THIS ROLE
_____

| WHAT I ENJOYED MOST ABOUT THIS ROLE TODAY | WHAT I WANT TO DO MORE OF IN THIS ROLE |

AREAS TO GROW
_____

Bedtime BRAIN DUMP

GAME PLAN FOR TOMORROW

I'M LOOKING FORWARD TO

ROLE CALL

Role _____

WHAT I AM GRATEFUL FOR ABOUT THIS ROLE
_____

WHAT I ENJOYED MOST ABOUT THIS ROLE TODAY

WHAT I WANT TO DO MORE OF IN THIS ROLE

AREAS TO GROW
_____

Role _____

WHAT I AM GRATEFUL FOR ABOUT THIS ROLE
_____

WHAT I ENJOYED MOST ABOUT THIS ROLE TODAY

WHAT I WANT TO DO MORE OF IN THIS ROLE

AREAS TO GROW
_____

Role _____

WHAT I AM GRATEFUL FOR ABOUT THIS ROLE
_____

WHAT I ENJOYED MOST ABOUT THIS ROLE TODAY

WHAT I WANT TO DO MORE OF IN THIS ROLE

AREAS TO GROW
_____

Role _____

WHAT I AM GRATEFUL FOR ABOUT THIS ROLE
_____

WHAT I ENJOYED MOST ABOUT THIS ROLE TODAY

WHAT I WANT TO DO MORE OF IN THIS ROLE

AREAS TO GROW
_____

Role _____

WHAT I AM GRATEFUL FOR ABOUT THIS ROLE
_____

WHAT I ENJOYED MOST ABOUT THIS ROLE TODAY

WHAT I WANT TO DO MORE OF IN THIS ROLE

AREAS TO GROW
_____

Bedtime BRAIN DUMP

- [ ] _____
- [ ] _____
- [ ] _____
- [ ] _____
- [ ] _____
- [ ] _____
- [ ] _____
- [ ] _____
- [ ] _____
- [ ] _____
- [ ] _____
- [ ] _____
- [ ] _____

GAME PLAN FOR TOMORROW

_____
_____
_____
_____
_____
_____
_____
_____

I'M LOOKING FORWARD TO

_____
_____
_____
_____
_____
_____
_____
_____

ROLE CALL

Role _____

WHAT I AM GRATEFUL FOR ABOUT THIS ROLE
_____

WHAT I ENJOYED MOST ABOUT THIS ROLE TODAY

WHAT I WANT TO DO MORE OF IN THIS ROLE

AREAS TO GROW
_____

Role _____

WHAT I AM GRATEFUL FOR ABOUT THIS ROLE
_____

WHAT I ENJOYED MOST ABOUT THIS ROLE TODAY

WHAT I WANT TO DO MORE OF IN THIS ROLE

AREAS TO GROW
_____

Role _____

WHAT I AM GRATEFUL FOR ABOUT THIS ROLE
_____

WHAT I ENJOYED MOST ABOUT THIS ROLE TODAY

WHAT I WANT TO DO MORE OF IN THIS ROLE

AREAS TO GROW
_____

Role _____

WHAT I AM GRATEFUL FOR ABOUT THIS ROLE
_____

WHAT I ENJOYED MOST ABOUT THIS ROLE TODAY

WHAT I WANT TO DO MORE OF IN THIS ROLE

AREAS TO GROW
_____

Role _____

WHAT I AM GRATEFUL FOR ABOUT THIS ROLE
_____

WHAT I ENJOYED MOST ABOUT THIS ROLE TODAY

WHAT I WANT TO DO MORE OF IN THIS ROLE

AREAS TO GROW
_____

Bedtime BRAIN DUMP

GAME PLAN FOR TOMORROW

I'M LOOKING FORWARD TO

ROLE CALL

Role _____

WHAT I AM GRATEFUL FOR ABOUT THIS ROLE
_____

WHAT I ENJOYED MOST ABOUT THIS ROLE TODAY

WHAT I WANT TO DO MORE OF IN THIS ROLE

AREAS TO GROW
_____

Role _____

WHAT I AM GRATEFUL FOR ABOUT THIS ROLE
_____

WHAT I ENJOYED MOST ABOUT THIS ROLE TODAY

WHAT I WANT TO DO MORE OF IN THIS ROLE

AREAS TO GROW
_____

Role _____

WHAT I AM GRATEFUL FOR ABOUT THIS ROLE
_____

WHAT I ENJOYED MOST ABOUT THIS ROLE TODAY

WHAT I WANT TO DO MORE OF IN THIS ROLE

AREAS TO GROW
_____

Role _____

WHAT I AM GRATEFUL FOR ABOUT THIS ROLE
_____

WHAT I ENJOYED MOST ABOUT THIS ROLE TODAY

WHAT I WANT TO DO MORE OF IN THIS ROLE

AREAS TO GROW
_____

Role _____

WHAT I AM GRATEFUL FOR ABOUT THIS ROLE
_____

WHAT I ENJOYED MOST ABOUT THIS ROLE TODAY

WHAT I WANT TO DO MORE OF IN THIS ROLE

AREAS TO GROW
_____

Bedtime BRAIN DUMP

GAME PLAN FOR TOMORROW

I'M LOOKING FORWARD TO

ROLE CALL

Role _____

WHAT I AM GRATEFUL FOR ABOUT THIS ROLE
_____

| WHAT I ENJOYED MOST ABOUT THIS ROLE TODAY | WHAT I WANT TO DO MORE OF IN THIS ROLE |

AREAS TO GROW
_____

Role _____

WHAT I AM GRATEFUL FOR ABOUT THIS ROLE
_____

| WHAT I ENJOYED MOST ABOUT THIS ROLE TODAY | WHAT I WANT TO DO MORE OF IN THIS ROLE |

AREAS TO GROW
_____

Role _____

WHAT I AM GRATEFUL FOR ABOUT THIS ROLE
_____

| WHAT I ENJOYED MOST ABOUT THIS ROLE TODAY | WHAT I WANT TO DO MORE OF IN THIS ROLE |

AREAS TO GROW
_____

Role _____

WHAT I AM GRATEFUL FOR ABOUT THIS ROLE
_____

| WHAT I ENJOYED MOST ABOUT THIS ROLE TODAY | WHAT I WANT TO DO MORE OF IN THIS ROLE |

AREAS TO GROW
_____

Role _____

WHAT I AM GRATEFUL FOR ABOUT THIS ROLE
_____

| WHAT I ENJOYED MOST ABOUT THIS ROLE TODAY | WHAT I WANT TO DO MORE OF IN THIS ROLE |

AREAS TO GROW
_____

Bedtime BRAIN DUMP

GAME PLAN FOR TOMORROW

I'M LOOKING FORWARD TO

ROLE CALL

Role _____

WHAT I AM GRATEFUL FOR ABOUT THIS ROLE
_____

WHAT I ENJOYED MOST ABOUT THIS ROLE TODAY

WHAT I WANT TO DO MORE OF IN THIS ROLE

AREAS TO GROW
_____

Role _____

WHAT I AM GRATEFUL FOR ABOUT THIS ROLE
_____

WHAT I ENJOYED MOST ABOUT THIS ROLE TODAY

WHAT I WANT TO DO MORE OF IN THIS ROLE

AREAS TO GROW
_____

Role _____

WHAT I AM GRATEFUL FOR ABOUT THIS ROLE
_____

WHAT I ENJOYED MOST ABOUT THIS ROLE TODAY

WHAT I WANT TO DO MORE OF IN THIS ROLE

AREAS TO GROW
_____

Role _____

WHAT I AM GRATEFUL FOR ABOUT THIS ROLE
_____

WHAT I ENJOYED MOST ABOUT THIS ROLE TODAY

WHAT I WANT TO DO MORE OF IN THIS ROLE

AREAS TO GROW
_____

Role _____

WHAT I AM GRATEFUL FOR ABOUT THIS ROLE
_____

WHAT I ENJOYED MOST ABOUT THIS ROLE TODAY

WHAT I WANT TO DO MORE OF IN THIS ROLE

AREAS TO GROW
_____

Bedtime BRAIN DUMP

- ☐ _____
- ☐ _____
- ☐ _____
- ☐ _____
- ☐ _____
- ☐ _____
- ☐ _____
- ☐ _____
- ☐ _____
- ☐ _____
- ☐ _____
- ☐ _____
- ☐ _____

GAME PLAN FOR TOMORROW

_____
_____
_____
_____
_____
_____
_____
_____

I'M LOOKING FORWARD TO

_____
_____
_____
_____
_____
_____
_____
_____

ROLE CALL

Role _____

WHAT I AM GRATEFUL FOR ABOUT THIS ROLE
_____

WHAT I ENJOYED MOST ABOUT THIS ROLE TODAY

WHAT I WANT TO DO MORE OF IN THIS ROLE

AREAS TO GROW
_____

Role _____

WHAT I AM GRATEFUL FOR ABOUT THIS ROLE
_____

WHAT I ENJOYED MOST ABOUT THIS ROLE TODAY

WHAT I WANT TO DO MORE OF IN THIS ROLE

AREAS TO GROW
_____

Role _____

WHAT I AM GRATEFUL FOR ABOUT THIS ROLE
_____

WHAT I ENJOYED MOST ABOUT THIS ROLE TODAY

WHAT I WANT TO DO MORE OF IN THIS ROLE

AREAS TO GROW
_____

Role _____

WHAT I AM GRATEFUL FOR ABOUT THIS ROLE
_____

WHAT I ENJOYED MOST ABOUT THIS ROLE TODAY

WHAT I WANT TO DO MORE OF IN THIS ROLE

ARFAS TO GROW
_____

Role _____

WHAT I AM GRATEFUL FOR ABOUT THIS ROLE
_____

WHAT I ENJOYED MOST ABOUT THIS ROLE TODAY

WHAT I WANT TO DO MORE OF IN THIS ROLE

AREAS TO GROW
_____

Bedtime BRAIN DUMP

GAME PLAN FOR TOMORROW

I'M LOOKING FORWARD TO

ROLE CALL

Role _____   WHAT I AM GRATEFUL FOR ABOUT THIS ROLE
_____

| WHAT I ENJOYED MOST ABOUT THIS ROLE TODAY | WHAT I WANT TO DO MORE OF IN THIS ROLE |

AREAS TO GROW
_____

Role _____   WHAT I AM GRATEFUL FOR ABOUT THIS ROLE
_____

| WHAT I ENJOYED MOST ABOUT THIS ROLE TODAY | WHAT I WANT TO DO MORE OF IN THIS ROLE |

AREAS TO GROW
_____

Role _____   WHAT I AM GRATEFUL FOR ABOUT THIS ROLE
_____

| WHAT I ENJOYED MOST ABOUT THIS ROLE TODAY | WHAT I WANT TO DO MORE OF IN THIS ROLE |

AREAS TO GROW
_____

Role _____   WHAT I AM GRATEFUL FOR ABOUT THIS ROLE
_____

| WHAT I ENJOYED MOST ABOUT THIS ROLE TODAY | WHAT I WANT TO DO MORE OF IN THIS ROLE |

AREAS TO GROW
_____

Role _____   WHAT I AM GRATEFUL FOR ABOUT THIS ROLE
_____

| WHAT I ENJOYED MOST ABOUT THIS ROLE TODAY | WHAT I WANT TO DO MORE OF IN THIS ROLE |

AREAS TO GROW
_____

Bedtime BRAIN DUMP

GAME PLAN FOR TOMORROW

I'M LOOKING FORWARD TO

ROLE CALL

Role _____

WHAT I AM GRATEFUL FOR ABOUT THIS ROLE
_____

WHAT I ENJOYED MOST ABOUT THIS ROLE TODAY

WHAT I WANT TO DO MORE OF IN THIS ROLE

AREAS TO GROW
_____

Role _____

WHAT I AM GRATEFUL FOR ABOUT THIS ROLE
_____

WHAT I ENJOYED MOST ABOUT THIS ROLE TODAY

WHAT I WANT TO DO MORE OF IN THIS ROLE

AREAS TO GROW
_____

Role _____

WHAT I AM GRATEFUL FOR ABOUT THIS ROLE
_____

WHAT I ENJOYED MOST ABOUT THIS ROLE TODAY

WHAT I WANT TO DO MORE OF IN THIS ROLE

AREAS TO GROW
_____

Role _____

WHAT I AM GRATEFUL FOR ABOUT THIS ROLE
_____

WHAT I ENJOYED MOST ABOUT THIS ROLE TODAY

WHAT I WANT TO DO MORE OF IN THIS ROLE

AREAS TO GROW
_____

Role _____

WHAT I AM GRATEFUL FOR ABOUT THIS ROLE
_____

WHAT I ENJOYED MOST ABOUT THIS ROLE TODAY

WHAT I WANT TO DO MORE OF IN THIS ROLE

AREAS TO GROW
_____

Bedtime BRAIN DUMP

GAME PLAN FOR TOMORROW

I'M LOOKING FORWARD TO

ROLE CALL

Role _____ WHAT I AM GRATEFUL FOR ABOUT THIS ROLE
_____

| WHAT I ENJOYED MOST ABOUT THIS ROLE TODAY | WHAT I WANT TO DO MORE OF IN THIS ROLE |

AREAS TO GROW
_____

Role _____ WHAT I AM GRATEFUL FOR ABOUT THIS ROLE
_____

| WHAT I ENJOYED MOST ABOUT THIS ROLE TODAY | WHAT I WANT TO DO MORE OF IN THIS ROLE |

AREAS TO GROW
_____

Role _____ WHAT I AM GRATEFUL FOR ABOUT THIS ROLE
_____

| WHAT I ENJOYED MOST ABOUT THIS ROLE TODAY | WHAT I WANT TO DO MORE OF IN THIS ROLE |

AREAS TO GROW
_____

Role _____ WHAT I AM GRATEFUL FOR ABOUT THIS ROLE
_____

| WHAT I ENJOYED MOST ABOUT THIS ROLE TODAY | WHAT I WANT TO DO MORE OF IN THIS ROLE |

AREAS TO GROW
_____

Role _____ WHAT I AM GRATEFUL FOR ABOUT THIS ROLE
_____

| WHAT I ENJOYED MOST ABOUT THIS ROLE TODAY | WHAT I WANT TO DO MORE OF IN THIS ROLE |

AREAS TO GROW
_____

Bedtime BRAIN DUMP

GAME PLAN FOR TOMORROW

I'M LOOKING FORWARD TO

ROLE CALL

Role _____

WHAT I AM GRATEFUL FOR ABOUT THIS ROLE
_____

WHAT I ENJOYED MOST ABOUT THIS ROLE TODAY

WHAT I WANT TO DO MORE OF IN THIS ROLE

AREAS TO GROW
_____

Role _____

WHAT I AM GRATEFUL FOR ABOUT THIS ROLE
_____

WHAT I ENJOYED MOST ABOUT THIS ROLE TODAY

WHAT I WANT TO DO MORE OF IN THIS ROLE

AREAS TO GROW
_____

Role _____

WHAT I AM GRATEFUL FOR ABOUT THIS ROLE
_____

WHAT I ENJOYED MOST ABOUT THIS ROLE TODAY

WHAT I WANT TO DO MORE OF IN THIS ROLE

AREAS TO GROW
_____

Role _____

WHAT I AM GRATEFUL FOR ABOUT THIS ROLE
_____

WHAT I ENJOYED MOST ABOUT THIS ROLE TODAY

WHAT I WANT TO DO MORE OF IN THIS ROLE

AREAS TO GROW
_____

Role _____

WHAT I AM GRATEFUL FOR ABOUT THIS ROLE
_____

WHAT I ENJOYED MOST ABOUT THIS ROLE TODAY

WHAT I WANT TO DO MORE OF IN THIS ROLE

AREAS TO GROW
_____

Bedtime BRAIN DUMP

- _____
- _____
- _____
- _____
- _____
- _____
- _____
- _____
- _____
- _____
- _____
- _____
- _____
- _____

GAME PLAN FOR TOMORROW

_____
_____
_____
_____
_____
_____
_____

I'M LOOKING FORWARD TO

_____
_____
_____
_____
_____
_____
_____

ROLE CALL

Role _____

WHAT I AM GRATEFUL FOR ABOUT THIS ROLE
_____

WHAT I ENJOYED MOST ABOUT THIS ROLE TODAY

WHAT I WANT TO DO MORE OF IN THIS ROLE

AREAS TO GROW
_____

Role _____

WHAT I AM GRATEFUL FOR ABOUT THIS ROLE
_____

WHAT I ENJOYED MOST ABOUT THIS ROLE TODAY

WHAT I WANT TO DO MORE OF IN THIS ROLE

AREAS TO GROW
_____

Role _____

WHAT I AM GRATEFUL FOR ABOUT THIS ROLE
_____

WHAT I ENJOYED MOST ABOUT THIS ROLE TODAY

WHAT I WANT TO DO MORE OF IN THIS ROLE

AREAS TO GROW
_____

Role _____

WHAT I AM GRATEFUL FOR ABOUT THIS ROLE
_____

WHAT I ENJOYED MOST ABOUT THIS ROLE TODAY

WHAT I WANT TO DO MORE OF IN THIS ROLE

AREAS TO GROW
_____

Role _____

WHAT I AM GRATEFUL FOR ABOUT THIS ROLE
_____

WHAT I ENJOYED MOST ABOUT THIS ROLE TODAY

WHAT I WANT TO DO MORE OF IN THIS ROLE

AREAS TO GROW
_____

Bedtime BRAIN DUMP

- ☐ _____
- ☐ _____
- ☐ _____
- ☐ _____
- ☐ _____
- ☐ _____
- ☐ _____
- ☐ _____
- ☐ _____
- ☐ _____
- ☐ _____
- ☐ _____
- ☐ _____

GAME PLAN FOR TOMORROW

_____
_____
_____
_____
_____
_____
_____

I'M LOOKING FORWARD TO

_____
_____
_____
_____
_____
_____
_____

ROLE CALL

Role _____

WHAT I AM GRATEFUL FOR ABOUT THIS ROLE
_____

WHAT I ENJOYED MOST ABOUT THIS ROLE TODAY

WHAT I WANT TO DO MORE OF IN THIS ROLE

AREAS TO GROW
_____

Role _____

WHAT I AM GRATEFUL FOR ABOUT THIS ROLE
_____

WHAT I ENJOYED MOST ABOUT THIS ROLE TODAY

WHAT I WANT TO DO MORE OF IN THIS ROLE

AREAS TO GROW
_____

Role _____

WHAT I AM GRATEFUL FOR ABOUT THIS ROLE
_____

WHAT I ENJOYED MOST ABOUT THIS ROLE TODAY

WHAT I WANT TO DO MORE OF IN THIS ROLE

AREAS TO GROW
_____

Role _____

WHAT I AM GRATEFUL FOR ABOUT THIS ROLE
_____

WHAT I ENJOYED MOST ABOUT THIS ROLE TODAY

WHAT I WANT TO DO MORE OF IN THIS ROLE

AREAS TO GROW
_____

Role _____

WHAT I AM GRATEFUL FOR ABOUT THIS ROLE
_____

WHAT I ENJOYED MOST ABOUT THIS ROLE TODAY

WHAT I WANT TO DO MORE OF IN THIS ROLE

AREAS TO GROW
_____

Bedtime BRAIN DUMP

GAME PLAN FOR TOMORROW

I'M LOOKING FORWARD TO

ROLE CALL

Role _____

WHAT I AM GRATEFUL FOR ABOUT THIS ROLE
_____

WHAT I ENJOYED MOST ABOUT THIS ROLE TODAY

WHAT I WANT TO DO MORE OF IN THIS ROLE

AREAS TO GROW
_____

Role _____

WHAT I AM GRATEFUL FOR ABOUT THIS ROLE
_____

WHAT I ENJOYED MOST ABOUT THIS ROLE TODAY

WHAT I WANT TO DO MORE OF IN THIS ROLE

AREAS TO GROW
_____

Role _____

WHAT I AM GRATEFUL FOR ABOUT THIS ROLE
_____

WHAT I ENJOYED MOST ABOUT THIS ROLE TODAY

WHAT I WANT TO DO MORE OF IN THIS ROLE

AREAS TO GROW
_____

Role _____

WHAT I AM GRATEFUL FOR ABOUT THIS ROLE
_____

WHAT I ENJOYED MOST ABOUT THIS ROLE TODAY

WHAT I WANT TO DO MORE OF IN THIS ROLE

AREAS TO GROW
_____

Role _____

WHAT I AM GRATEFUL FOR ABOUT THIS ROLE
_____

WHAT I ENJOYED MOST ABOUT THIS ROLE TODAY

WHAT I WANT TO DO MORE OF IN THIS ROLE

AREAS TO GROW
_____

Bedtime BRAIN DUMP

- [ ] _____
- [ ] _____
- [ ] _____
- [ ] _____
- [ ] _____
- [ ] _____
- [ ] _____
- [ ] _____
- [ ] _____
- [ ] _____
- [ ] _____
- [ ] _____
- [ ] _____

GAME PLAN FOR TOMORROW

_____
_____
_____
_____
_____
_____
_____
_____

I'M LOOKING FORWARD TO

_____
_____
_____
_____
_____
_____
_____
_____

ROLE CALL

Role _____

WHAT I AM GRATEFUL FOR ABOUT THIS ROLE
_____

WHAT I ENJOYED MOST ABOUT THIS ROLE TODAY

WHAT I WANT TO DO MORE OF IN THIS ROLE

AREAS TO GROW
_____

Role _____

WHAT I AM GRATEFUL FOR ABOUT THIS ROLE
_____

WHAT I ENJOYED MOST ABOUT THIS ROLE TODAY

WHAT I WANT TO DO MORE OF IN THIS ROLE

AREAS TO GROW
_____

Role _____

WHAT I AM GRATEFUL FOR ABOUT THIS ROLE
_____

WHAT I ENJOYED MOST ABOUT THIS ROLE TODAY

WHAT I WANT TO DO MORE OF IN THIS ROLE

AREAS TO GROW
_____

Role _____

WHAT I AM GRATEFUL FOR ABOUT THIS ROLE
_____

WHAT I ENJOYED MOST ABOUT THIS ROLE TODAY

WHAT I WANT TO DO MORE OF IN THIS ROLE

AREAS TO GROW
_____

Role _____

WHAT I AM GRATEFUL FOR ABOUT THIS ROLE
_____

WHAT I ENJOYED MOST ABOUT THIS ROLE TODAY

WHAT I WANT TO DO MORE OF IN THIS ROLE

AREAS TO GROW
_____

Bedtime BRAIN DUMP

☐ _____
☐ _____
☐ _____
☐ _____
☐ _____
☐ _____
☐ _____
☐ _____
☐ _____
☐ _____
☐ _____
☐ _____
☐ _____

GAME PLAN FOR TOMORROW

_____
_____
_____
_____
_____
_____
_____

I'M LOOKING FORWARD TO

_____
_____
_____
_____
_____
_____
_____

ROLE CALL

Role _____ WHAT I AM GRATEFUL FOR ABOUT THIS ROLE
_____

WHAT I ENJOYED MOST ABOUT THIS ROLE TODAY | WHAT I WANT TO DO MORE OF IN THIS ROLE

AREAS TO GROW
_____

Role _____ WHAT I AM GRATEFUL FOR ABOUT THIS ROLE
_____

WHAT I ENJOYED MOST ABOUT THIS ROLE TODAY | WHAT I WANT TO DO MORE OF IN THIS ROLE

AREAS TO GROW
_____

Role _____ WHAT I AM GRATEFUL FOR ABOUT THIS ROLE
_____

WHAT I ENJOYED MOST ABOUT THIS ROLE TODAY | WHAT I WANT TO DO MORE OF IN THIS ROLE

AREAS TO GROW
_____

Role _____ WHAT I AM GRATEFUL FOR ABOUT THIS ROLE
_____

WHAT I ENJOYED MOST ABOUT THIS ROLE TODAY | WHAT I WANT TO DO MORE OF IN THIS ROLE

AREAS TO GROW
_____

Role _____ WHAT I AM GRATEFUL FOR ABOUT THIS ROLE
_____

WHAT I ENJOYED MOST ABOUT THIS ROLE TODAY | WHAT I WANT TO DO MORE OF IN THIS ROLE

AREAS TO GROW
_____

Bedtime BRAIN DUMP

- _____
- _____
- _____
- _____
- _____
- _____
- _____
- _____
- _____
- _____
- _____
- _____
- _____

GAME PLAN FOR TOMORROW

_____
_____
_____
_____
_____
_____
_____
_____

I'M LOOKING FORWARD TO

_____
_____
_____
_____
_____
_____
_____
_____

ROLE CALL

Role _____

WHAT I AM GRATEFUL FOR ABOUT THIS ROLE
_____

WHAT I ENJOYED MOST ABOUT THIS ROLE TODAY | WHAT I WANT TO DO MORE OF IN THIS ROLE

AREAS TO GROW
_____

Role _____

WHAT I AM GRATEFUL FOR ABOUT THIS ROLE
_____

WHAT I ENJOYED MOST ABOUT THIS ROLE TODAY | WHAT I WANT TO DO MORE OF IN THIS ROLE

AREAS TO GROW
_____

Role _____

WHAT I AM GRATEFUL FOR ABOUT THIS ROLE
_____

WHAT I ENJOYED MOST ABOUT THIS ROLE TODAY | WHAT I WANT TO DO MORE OF IN THIS ROLE

AREAS TO GROW
_____

Role _____

WHAT I AM GRATEFUL FOR ABOUT THIS ROLE
_____

WHAT I ENJOYED MOST ABOUT THIS ROLE TODAY | WHAT I WANT TO DO MORE OF IN THIS ROLE

AREAS TO GROW
_____

Role _____

WHAT I AM GRATEFUL FOR ABOUT THIS ROLE
_____

WHAT I ENJOYED MOST ABOUT THIS ROLE TODAY | WHAT I WANT TO DO MORE OF IN THIS ROLE

AREAS TO GROW
_____

Bedtime BRAIN DUMP

GAME PLAN FOR TOMORROW

I'M LOOKING FORWARD TO

ROLE CALL

Role _____
WHAT I AM GRATEFUL FOR ABOUT THIS ROLE
_____

WHAT I ENJOYED MOST ABOUT THIS ROLE TODAY

WHAT I WANT TO DO MORE OF IN THIS ROLE

AREAS TO GROW
_____

Role _____
WHAT I AM GRATEFUL FOR ABOUT THIS ROLE
_____

WHAT I ENJOYED MOST ABOUT THIS ROLE TODAY

WHAT I WANT TO DO MORE OF IN THIS ROLE

AREAS TO GROW
_____

Role _____
WHAT I AM GRATEFUL FOR ABOUT THIS ROLE
_____

WHAT I ENJOYED MOST ABOUT THIS ROLE TODAY

WHAT I WANT TO DO MORE OF IN THIS ROLE

AREAS TO GROW
_____

Role _____
WHAT I AM GRATEFUL FOR ABOUT THIS ROLE
_____

WHAT I ENJOYED MOST ABOUT THIS ROLE TODAY

WHAT I WANT TO DO MORE OF IN THIS ROLE

AREAS TO GROW
_____

Role _____
WHAT I AM GRATEFUL FOR ABOUT THIS ROLE
_____

WHAT I ENJOYED MOST ABOUT THIS ROLE TODAY

WHAT I WANT TO DO MORE OF IN THIS ROLE

AREAS TO GROW
_____

Bedtime BRAIN DUMP

- _____
- _____
- _____
- _____
- _____
- _____
- _____
- _____
- _____
- _____
- _____
- _____
- _____

GAME PLAN FOR TOMORROW

_____
_____
_____
_____
_____
_____
_____
_____

I'M LOOKING FORWARD TO

_____
_____
_____
_____
_____
_____
_____
_____

ROLE CALL

Role _____

WHAT I AM GRATEFUL FOR ABOUT THIS ROLE
_____

| WHAT I ENJOYED MOST ABOUT THIS ROLE TODAY | WHAT I WANT TO DO MORE OF IN THIS ROLE |

AREAS TO GROW
_____

Role _____

WHAT I AM GRATEFUL FOR ABOUT THIS ROLE
_____

| WHAT I ENJOYED MOST ABOUT THIS ROLE TODAY | WHAT I WANT TO DO MORE OF IN THIS ROLE |

AREAS TO GROW
_____

Role _____

WHAT I AM GRATEFUL FOR ABOUT THIS ROLE
_____

| WHAT I ENJOYED MOST ABOUT THIS ROLE TODAY | WHAT I WANT TO DO MORE OF IN THIS ROLE |

AREAS TO GROW
_____

Role _____

WHAT I AM GRATEFUL FOR ABOUT THIS ROLE
_____

| WHAT I ENJOYED MOST ABOUT THIS ROLE TODAY | WHAT I WANT TO DO MORE OF IN THIS ROLE |

AREAS TO GROW
_____

Role _____

WHAT I AM GRATEFUL FOR ABOUT THIS ROLE
_____

| WHAT I ENJOYED MOST ABOUT THIS ROLE TODAY | WHAT I WANT TO DO MORE OF IN THIS ROLE |

AREAS TO GROW
_____

Bedtime BRAIN DUMP

GAME PLAN FOR TOMORROW

I'M LOOKING FORWARD TO

ROLE CALL

Role _____

WHAT I AM GRATEFUL FOR ABOUT THIS ROLE
_____

WHAT I ENJOYED MOST ABOUT THIS ROLE TODAY

WHAT I WANT TO DO MORE OF IN THIS ROLE

AREAS TO GROW
_____

Role _____

WHAT I AM GRATEFUL FOR ABOUT THIS ROLE
_____

WHAT I ENJOYED MOST ABOUT THIS ROLE TODAY

WHAT I WANT TO DO MORE OF IN THIS ROLE

AREAS TO GROW
_____

Role _____

WHAT I AM GRATEFUL FOR ABOUT THIS ROLE
_____

WHAT I ENJOYED MOST ABOUT THIS ROLE TODAY

WHAT I WANT TO DO MORE OF IN THIS ROLE

AREAS TO GROW
_____

Role _____

WHAT I AM GRATEFUL FOR ABOUT THIS ROLE
_____

WHAT I ENJOYED MOST ABOUT THIS ROLE TODAY

WHAT I WANT TO DO MORE OF IN THIS ROLE

AREAS TO GROW
_____

Role _____

WHAT I AM GRATEFUL FOR ABOUT THIS ROLE
_____

WHAT I ENJOYED MOST ABOUT THIS ROLE TODAY

WHAT I WANT TO DO MORE OF IN THIS ROLE

AREAS TO GROW
_____

Bedtime BRAIN DUMP

GAME PLAN FOR TOMORROW

I'M LOOKING FORWARD TO

ROLE CALL

Role _____

WHAT I AM GRATEFUL FOR ABOUT THIS ROLE
_____

WHAT I ENJOYED MOST ABOUT THIS ROLE TODAY

WHAT I WANT TO DO MORE OF IN THIS ROLE

AREAS TO GROW
_____

Role _____

WHAT I AM GRATEFUL FOR ABOUT THIS ROLE
_____

WHAT I ENJOYED MOST ABOUT THIS ROLE TODAY

WHAT I WANT TO DO MORE OF IN THIS ROLE

AREAS TO GROW
_____

Role _____

WHAT I AM GRATEFUL FOR ABOUT THIS ROLE
_____

WHAT I ENJOYED MOST ABOUT THIS ROLE TODAY

WHAT I WANT TO DO MORE OF IN THIS ROLE

AREAS TO GROW
_____

Role _____

WHAT I AM GRATEFUL FOR ABOUT THIS ROLE
_____

WHAT I ENJOYED MOST ABOUT THIS ROLE TODAY

WHAT I WANT TO DO MORE OF IN THIS ROLE

AREAS TO GROW
_____

Role _____

WHAT I AM GRATEFUL FOR ABOUT THIS ROLE
_____

WHAT I ENJOYED MOST ABOUT THIS ROLE TODAY

WHAT I WANT TO DO MORE OF IN THIS ROLE

AREAS TO GROW
_____

Bedtime BRAIN DUMP

GAME PLAN FOR TOMORROW

I'M LOOKING FORWARD TO

ROLE CALL

Role _____ WHAT I AM GRATEFUL FOR ABOUT THIS ROLE
_____

WHAT I ENJOYED MOST ABOUT THIS ROLE TODAY | WHAT I WANT TO DO MORE OF IN THIS ROLE

AREAS TO GROW
_____

Role _____ WHAT I AM GRATEFUL FOR ABOUT THIS ROLE
_____

WHAT I ENJOYED MOST ABOUT THIS ROLE TODAY | WHAT I WANT TO DO MORE OF IN THIS ROLE

AREAS TO GROW
_____

Role _____ WHAT I AM GRATEFUL FOR ABOUT THIS ROLE
_____

WHAT I ENJOYED MOST ABOUT THIS ROLE TODAY | WHAT I WANT TO DO MORE OF IN THIS ROLE

AREAS TO GROW
_____

Role _____ WHAT I AM GRATEFUL FOR ABOUT THIS ROLE
_____

WHAT I ENJOYED MOST ABOUT THIS ROLE TODAY | WHAT I WANT TO DO MORE OF IN THIS ROLE

AREAS TO GROW
_____

Role _____ WHAT I AM GRATEFUL FOR ABOUT THIS ROLE
_____

WHAT I ENJOYED MOST ABOUT THIS ROLE TODAY | WHAT I WANT TO DO MORE OF IN THIS ROLE

AREAS TO GROW
_____

Bedtime BRAIN DUMP

- _____
- _____
- _____
- _____
- _____
- _____
- _____
- _____
- _____
- _____
- _____
- _____

GAME PLAN FOR TOMORROW

_____
_____
_____
_____
_____
_____
_____
_____

I'M LOOKING FORWARD TO

_____
_____
_____
_____
_____
_____
_____
_____

ROLE CALL

Role _____ WHAT I AM GRATEFUL FOR ABOUT THIS ROLE
_____

WHAT I ENJOYED MOST ABOUT THIS ROLE TODAY | WHAT I WANT TO DO MORE OF IN THIS ROLE

AREAS TO GROW
_____

Role _____ WHAT I AM GRATEFUL FOR ABOUT THIS ROLE
_____

WHAT I ENJOYED MOST ABOUT THIS ROLE TODAY | WHAT I WANT TO DO MORE OF IN THIS ROLE

AREAS TO GROW
_____

Role _____ WHAT I AM GRATEFUL FOR ABOUT THIS ROLE
_____

WHAT I ENJOYED MOST ABOUT THIS ROLE TODAY | WHAT I WANT TO DO MORE OF IN THIS ROLE

AREAS TO GROW
_____

Role _____ WHAT I AM GRATEFUL FOR ABOUT THIS ROLE
_____

WHAT I ENJOYED MOST ABOUT THIS ROLE TODAY | WHAT I WANT TO DO MORE OF IN THIS ROLE

AREAS TO GROW
_____

Role _____ WHAT I AM GRATEFUL FOR ABOUT THIS ROLE
_____

WHAT I ENJOYED MOST ABOUT THIS ROLE TODAY | WHAT I WANT TO DO MORE OF IN THIS ROLE

AREAS TO GROW
_____

Bedtime BRAIN DUMP

- _____
- _____
- _____
- _____
- _____
- _____
- _____
- _____
- _____
- _____
- _____
- _____
- _____
- _____

GAME PLAN FOR TOMORROW

_____
_____
_____
_____
_____
_____
_____

I'M LOOKING FORWARD TO

_____
_____
_____
_____
_____
_____
_____

ROLE CALL

Role _____ WHAT I AM GRATEFUL FOR ABOUT THIS ROLE
_____

| WHAT I ENJOYED MOST ABOUT THIS ROLE TODAY | WHAT I WANT TO DO MORE OF IN THIS ROLE |

AREAS TO GROW
_____

Role _____ WHAT I AM GRATEFUL FOR ABOUT THIS ROLE
_____

| WHAT I ENJOYED MOST ABOUT THIS ROLE TODAY | WHAT I WANT TO DO MORE OF IN THIS ROLE |

AREAS TO GROW
_____

Role _____ WHAT I AM GRATEFUL FOR ABOUT THIS ROLE
_____

| WHAT I ENJOYED MOST ABOUT THIS ROLE TODAY | WHAT I WANT TO DO MORE OF IN THIS ROLE |

AREAS TO GROW
_____

Role _____ WHAT I AM GRATEFUL FOR ABOUT THIS ROLE
_____

| WHAT I ENJOYED MOST ABOUT THIS ROLE TODAY | WHAT I WANT TO DO MORE OF IN THIS ROLE |

AREAS TO GROW
_____

Role _____ WHAT I AM GRATEFUL FOR ABOUT THIS ROLE
_____

| WHAT I ENJOYED MOST ABOUT THIS ROLE TODAY | WHAT I WANT TO DO MORE OF IN THIS ROLE |

AREAS TO GROW
_____

Bedtime BRAIN DUMP

- [ ] _____
- [ ] _____
- [ ] _____
- [ ] _____
- [ ] _____
- [ ] _____
- [ ] _____
- [ ] _____
- [ ] _____
- [ ] _____
- [ ] _____
- [ ] _____
- [ ] _____

GAME PLAN FOR TOMORROW

_____
_____
_____
_____
_____
_____
_____
_____

I'M LOOKING FORWARD TO

_____
_____
_____
_____
_____
_____
_____
_____

ROLE CALL

Role _____

WHAT I AM GRATEFUL FOR ABOUT THIS ROLE
_____

WHAT I ENJOYED MOST ABOUT THIS ROLE TODAY

WHAT I WANT TO DO MORE OF IN THIS ROLE

AREAS TO GROW
_____

Role _____

WHAT I AM GRATEFUL FOR ABOUT THIS ROLE
_____

WHAT I ENJOYED MOST ABOUT THIS ROLE TODAY

WHAT I WANT TO DO MORE OF IN THIS ROLE

AREAS TO GROW
_____

Role _____

WHAT I AM GRATEFUL FOR ABOUT THIS ROLE
_____

WHAT I ENJOYED MOST ABOUT THIS ROLE TODAY

WHAT I WANT TO DO MORE OF IN THIS ROLE

AREAS TO GROW
_____

Role _____

WHAT I AM GRATEFUL FOR ABOUT THIS ROLE
_____

WHAT I ENJOYED MOST ABOUT THIS ROLE TODAY

WHAT I WANT TO DO MORE OF IN THIS ROLE

AREAS TO GROW
_____

Role _____

WHAT I AM GRATEFUL FOR ABOUT THIS ROLE
_____

WHAT I ENJOYED MOST ABOUT THIS ROLE TODAY

WHAT I WANT TO DO MORE OF IN THIS ROLE

AREAS TO GROW
_____

Bedtime BRAIN DUMP

GAME PLAN FOR TOMORROW

I'M LOOKING FORWARD TO

ROLE CALL

Role _____ WHAT I AM GRATEFUL FOR ABOUT THIS ROLE
_____

| WHAT I ENJOYED MOST ABOUT THIS ROLE TODAY | WHAT I WANT TO DO MORE OF IN THIS ROLE |

AREAS TO GROW
_____

Role _____ WHAT I AM GRATEFUL FOR ABOUT THIS ROLE
_____

| WHAT I ENJOYED MOST ABOUT THIS ROLE TODAY | WHAT I WANT TO DO MORE OF IN THIS ROLE |

AREAS TO GROW
_____

Role _____ WHAT I AM GRATEFUL FOR ABOUT THIS ROLE
_____

| WHAT I ENJOYED MOST ABOUT THIS ROLE TODAY | WHAT I WANT TO DO MORE OF IN THIS ROLE |

AREAS TO GROW
_____

Role _____ WHAT I AM GRATEFUL FOR ABOUT THIS ROLE
_____

| WHAT I ENJOYED MOST ABOUT THIS ROLE TODAY | WHAT I WANT TO DO MORE OF IN THIS ROLE |

AREAS TO GROW
_____

Role _____ WHAT I AM GRATEFUL FOR ABOUT THIS ROLE
_____

| WHAT I ENJOYED MOST ABOUT THIS ROLE TODAY | WHAT I WANT TO DO MORE OF IN THIS ROLE |

AREAS TO GROW
_____

Bedtime BRAIN DUMP

- [ ] _____
- [ ] _____
- [ ] _____
- [ ] _____
- [ ] _____
- [ ] _____
- [ ] _____
- [ ] _____
- [ ] _____
- [ ] _____
- [ ] _____
- [ ] _____
- [ ] _____

GAME PLAN FOR TOMORROW

_____
_____
_____
_____
_____
_____
_____
_____

I'M LOOKING FORWARD TO

_____
_____
_____
_____
_____
_____
_____
_____

ROLE CALL

Role _____

WHAT I AM GRATEFUL FOR ABOUT THIS ROLE
_____

WHAT I ENJOYED MOST ABOUT THIS ROLE TODAY

WHAT I WANT TO DO MORE OF IN THIS ROLE

AREAS TO GROW
_____

Role _____

WHAT I AM GRATEFUL FOR ABOUT THIS ROLE
_____

WHAT I ENJOYED MOST ABOUT THIS ROLE TODAY

WHAT I WANT TO DO MORE OF IN THIS ROLE

AREAS TO GROW
_____

Role _____

WHAT I AM GRATEFUL FOR ABOUT THIS ROLE
_____

WHAT I ENJOYED MOST ABOUT THIS ROLE TODAY

WHAT I WANT TO DO MORE OF IN THIS ROLE

AREAS TO GROW
_____

Role _____

WHAT I AM GRATEFUL FOR ABOUT THIS ROLE
_____

WHAT I ENJOYED MOST ABOUT THIS ROLE TODAY

WHAT I WANT TO DO MORE OF IN THIS ROLE

AREAS TO GROW
_____

Role _____

WHAT I AM GRATEFUL FOR ABOUT THIS ROLE
_____

WHAT I ENJOYED MOST ABOUT THIS ROLE TODAY

WHAT I WANT TO DO MORE OF IN THIS ROLE

AREAS TO GROW
_____

Bedtime BRAIN DUMP

GAME PLAN FOR TOMORROW

I'M LOOKING FORWARD TO

ROLE CALL

Role _____ WHAT I AM GRATEFUL FOR ABOUT THIS ROLE
_____

WHAT I ENJOYED MOST ABOUT THIS ROLE TODAY | WHAT I WANT TO DO MORE OF IN THIS ROLE

AREAS TO GROW
_____

Role _____ WHAT I AM GRATEFUL FOR ABOUT THIS ROLE
_____

WHAT I ENJOYED MOST ABOUT THIS ROLE TODAY | WHAT I WANT TO DO MORE OF IN THIS ROLE

AREAS TO GROW
_____

Role _____ WHAT I AM GRATEFUL FOR ABOUT THIS ROLE
_____

WHAT I ENJOYED MOST ABOUT THIS ROLE TODAY | WHAT I WANT TO DO MORE OF IN THIS ROLE

AREAS TO GROW
_____

Role _____ WHAT I AM GRATEFUL FOR ABOUT THIS ROLE
_____

WHAT I ENJOYED MOST ABOUT THIS ROLE TODAY | WHAT I WANT TO DO MORE OF IN THIS ROLE

AREAS TO GROW
_____

Role _____ WHAT I AM GRATEFUL FOR ABOUT THIS ROLE
_____

WHAT I ENJOYED MOST ABOUT THIS ROLE TODAY | WHAT I WANT TO DO MORE OF IN THIS ROLE

AREAS TO GROW
_____

Bedtime BRAIN DUMP

- [ ] _____
- [ ] _____
- [ ] _____
- [ ] _____
- [ ] _____
- [ ] _____
- [ ] _____
- [ ] _____
- [ ] _____
- [ ] _____
- [ ] _____
- [ ] _____

GAME PLAN FOR TOMORROW

_____
_____
_____
_____
_____
_____
_____
_____

I'M LOOKING FORWARD TO

_____
_____
_____
_____
_____
_____
_____
_____

ROLE CALL

Role _____ WHAT I AM GRATEFUL FOR ABOUT THIS ROLE
_____

| WHAT I ENJOYED MOST ABOUT THIS ROLE TODAY | WHAT I WANT TO DO MORE OF IN THIS ROLE |

AREAS TO GROW
_____

Role _____ WHAT I AM GRATEFUL FOR ABOUT THIS ROLE
_____

| WHAT I ENJOYED MOST ABOUT THIS ROLE TODAY | WHAT I WANT TO DO MORE OF IN THIS ROLE |

AREAS TO GROW
_____

Role _____ WHAT I AM GRATEFUL FOR ABOUT THIS ROLE
_____

| WHAT I ENJOYED MOST ABOUT THIS ROLE TODAY | WHAT I WANT TO DO MORE OF IN THIS ROLE |

AREAS TO GROW
_____

Role _____ WHAT I AM GRATEFUL FOR ABOUT THIS ROLE
_____

| WHAT I ENJOYED MOST ABOUT THIS ROLE TODAY | WHAT I WANT TO DO MORE OF IN THIS ROLE |

AREAS TO GROW
_____

Role _____ WHAT I AM GRATEFUL FOR ABOUT THIS ROLE
_____

| WHAT I ENJOYED MOST ABOUT THIS ROLE TODAY | WHAT I WANT TO DO MORE OF IN THIS ROLE |

AREAS TO GROW
_____

Bedtime BRAIN DUMP

- _____
- _____
- _____
- _____
- _____
- _____
- _____
- _____
- _____
- _____
- _____
- _____
- _____
- _____
- _____

GAME PLAN FOR TOMORROW

_____
_____
_____
_____
_____
_____
_____

I'M LOOKING FORWARD TO

_____
_____
_____
_____
_____
_____
_____

ROLE CALL

Role _____

WHAT I AM GRATEFUL FOR ABOUT THIS ROLE
_____

WHAT I ENJOYED MOST ABOUT THIS ROLE TODAY

WHAT I WANT TO DO MORE OF IN THIS ROLE

AREAS TO GROW
_____

Role _____

WHAT I AM GRATEFUL FOR ABOUT THIS ROLE
_____

WHAT I ENJOYED MOST ABOUT THIS ROLE TODAY

WHAT I WANT TO DO MORE OF IN THIS ROLE

AREAS TO GROW
_____

Role _____

WHAT I AM GRATEFUL FOR ABOUT THIS ROLE
_____

WHAT I ENJOYED MOST ABOUT THIS ROLE TODAY

WHAT I WANT TO DO MORE OF IN THIS ROLE

AREAS TO GROW
_____

Role _____

WHAT I AM GRATEFUL FOR ABOUT THIS ROLE
_____

WHAT I ENJOYED MOST ABOUT THIS ROLE TODAY

WHAT I WANT TO DO MORE OF IN THIS ROLE

AREAS TO GROW
_____

Role _____

WHAT I AM GRATEFUL FOR ABOUT THIS ROLE
_____

WHAT I ENJOYED MOST ABOUT THIS ROLE TODAY

WHAT I WANT TO DO MORE OF IN THIS ROLE

AREAS TO GROW
_____

Bedtime BRAIN DUMP

- _____
- _____
- _____
- _____
- _____
- _____
- _____
- _____
- _____
- _____
- _____
- _____
- _____

GAME PLAN FOR TOMORROW

_____
_____
_____
_____
_____
_____
_____

I'M LOOKING FORWARD TO

_____
_____
_____
_____
_____
_____
_____

ROLE CALL

Role _____ WHAT I AM GRATEFUL FOR ABOUT THIS ROLE
_____

WHAT I ENJOYED MOST ABOUT THIS ROLE TODAY | WHAT I WANT TO DO MORE OF IN THIS ROLE

AREAS TO GROW
_____

Role _____ WHAT I AM GRATEFUL FOR ABOUT THIS ROLE
_____

WHAT I ENJOYED MOST ABOUT THIS ROLE TODAY | WHAT I WANT TO DO MORE OF IN THIS ROLE

AREAS TO GROW
_____

Role _____ WHAT I AM GRATEFUL FOR ABOUT THIS ROLE
_____

WHAT I ENJOYED MOST ABOUT THIS ROLE TODAY | WHAT I WANT TO DO MORE OF IN THIS ROLE

AREAS TO GROW
_____

Role _____ WHAT I AM GRATEFUL FOR ABOUT THIS ROLE
_____

WHAT I ENJOYED MOST ABOUT THIS ROLE TODAY | WHAT I WANT TO DO MORE OF IN THIS ROLE

AREAS TO GROW
_____

Role _____ WHAT I AM GRATEFUL FOR ABOUT THIS ROLE
_____

WHAT I ENJOYED MOST ABOUT THIS ROLE TODAY | WHAT I WANT TO DO MORE OF IN THIS ROLE

AREAS TO GROW
_____

Bedtime BRAIN DUMP

GAME PLAN FOR TOMORROW

I'M LOOKING FORWARD TO

90
DAYS

Nothing can stop you now!

Hey babe,

Big congrats on making it through all 90 days! Are you ready to take the next step to level up your business? Then join us in **The Coach Collection** Membership to get access to all of our tips, templates and resources to help you maximize the pockets of time you have in your busy schedule.

To join, visit
www.shecollectivecompany.com
and look for "membership"

Made in the USA
Monee, IL
08 December 2021